MW00462375

THE BEST
GAME EVER

THE BEST GAME EVER

How Frank McGuire's '57 Tar Heels Beat Wilt and
Revolutionized College Basketball

ADAM LUCAS

LYONS PRESS
Guilford, Connecticut
An imprint of Globe Pequot Press

To buy books in quantity for corporate use
or incentives, call **(800) 962-0973**
or e-mail **premiums@GlobePequot.com.**

Copyright © 2006 by Tobacco Road Media, Inc.
First Lyons Press paperback edition, 2012

ALL RIGHTS RESERVED. No part of this book may be reproduced
or transmitted in any form by any means, electronic or mechanical,
including photocopying and recording, or by any information storage and
retrieval system, except as may be expressly permitted in writing from the
publisher. Requests for permission should be addressed to Globe Pequot
Press, Attn: Rights and Permissions Department, P.O. Box 480, Guilford,
CT 06437.

Lyons Press is an imprint of Globe Pequot Press.

Library of Congress Cataloging-in-Publication Data is available on file.

ISBN 978-0-7627-7427-2

Printed in the United States of America

10 9 8 7 6 5 4 3 2 1

For Stephanie, McKay, and Asher, who understand that I have to spend some nights writing books when I would rather be reading them.

Contents

Foreword

I was just six years old when Frank McGuire and his 1957 Tar Heels made their magical run to the national championship.

Of course, it's only in hindsight that I know it was a magical run. At the time, growing up in Asheville, I knew very little about Atlantic Coast Conference basketball. We didn't have two games on ESPN every weeknight and three on Saturday—we didn't even have one game on television. To be honest, at that age I was more into baseball than basketball. My buddies and I would play baseball most every day, and it wasn't until the seventh grade that basketball began to interest me.

What I know today is that the 1957 team fostered a lot of the now-constant hysteria in North Carolina about the game of college basketball. They also helped create opportunities for people like me who have been lucky enough to spend their lives in the game.

Over the years, I have had the opportunity to get to know many members of the 1957 team. Their championship season may have been more than five decades ago, but it is still so relevant today. I remember watching Melvin Scott shoot free throws against Villanova in the regional semifinals in 2005. They were big shots—we were up by only 2 points with 28.9 seconds left in the game. For some reason I looked at Melvin's feet when he was at the line. When he shot the ball, he went all the way up on his toes and followed through. I remembered hearing some of the 1957 players—especially Joe Quigg, who made the clinching free throws in the championship game—talk about how assistant coach Buck Freeman always told them to finish on their toes. When I saw Melvin finish on his toes, I felt really good about those free throws.

What strikes me is how much of a big-time team the 1957 squad was then—and still is today. My first year as head coach at Carolina, we had a reunion of all our lettermen. Four of the five starters from the '57 team were there. It was really impressive how much they still act like a team. The relationships they have and the memories they share are some of the strongest things about them, even more than 50 years after they won a championship together.

This type of bond is exactly what I talk about with current players—that when their careers are over, they won't remember how many points they scored or how many rebounds they got on a specific night as individuals. They will remember the *team* accomplishments. That's why I brought up 1957 before our team took the floor against Illinois in the 2005 championship game. I told our guys, "You have a chance to have that same feeling as those players from 1957. You can do this tonight. You can have those relationships and those memories 50 years from now."

We were able to make new memories that April night in St. Louis. I've enjoyed wearing the championship ring and looking at the banner in the Smith Center. But it's even more special to know that that particular group of players will have a unique bond for as long as they live.

The game was different in 1957; the amount of national attention was different; the television coverage was different. But no matter what the era, a big-time team is always going to be a big-time team. And the 1957 North Carolina Tar Heels were the original big-time team.

—Roy Williams

Acknowledgments

Through the course of researching this book, I met many people who saw numerous games during the 1956–57 season. I was not one of them.

That made the writing of this book a unique project for me. For past books I mainly watched events unfold and then chronicled them. For this one I was much more reliant on the memories of other people, and I leaned on them to reconstruct events. Sometimes—many times—memories conflicted, and that was part of the fun of piecing together this amazing year in North Carolina athletics history.

The 1956–57 Tar Heels played the biggest role in helping me write this book. My firsthand interviews with Pete Brennan, Bob Cunningham, Joel Fleishman, Tommy Kearns, Danny Lotz, Joe Quigg, Lennie Rosenbluth, and Bob Young provided a picture of the era that otherwise would have been unavailable. Lennie Rosenbluth and his wife, Pat, deserve special mention, as they were extremely supportive of the project from the first time I mentioned it, in March 2003. In many ways players on the 1957 championship team have stood in the shadows of Carolina basketball, behind some other very worthy teams. To their credit they haven't spent much time complaining about the slight. Hopefully this book will help them get a little of the attention they deserve.

Other people in and around Carolina during the Frank McGuire era were also very helpful. Ben Lubin painted a broader picture of the McGuire/Rosenbluth relationship, and Buzz Merritt provided insight on the journalistic mechanics of covering the Tar Heels in 1957.

From the beginning I thought this was more than just a basketball story. It is also about the way the 1956–57 season changed sports culture in the state of North Carolina. To that end, Chuck Davenport (who also pored over an early draft, providing valuable advice), Alfred Hamilton, Cobby Reaves, Roy High, Jack Hilliard, Louie Rosenstock, Clark Smith, and Francho Palmer were candid about their experiences as fans. Frank Deford generously gave of his time one fall afternoon in New York City and provided his trademark slice of insight and wit. Another New York City icon, Howard Garfinkel, helped explain the role of talent evaluators.

My first interview for this book was also one of my most productive, as Woody Durham described the way the 1956–57 team captured his imagination as a fan. He also handed over his complete file on the team for the duration of the project. (For a writer this is akin to being a physics buff who is granted unlimited access to Stephen Hawking's notes.)

Not everything about this team could be gathered from interviews. A significant amount of library research was needed—a scary proposition to someone like me who has tried to avoid the library his whole life. Jason Tomberlin, who works with the Carolina Collection on the UNC campus, simplified my task by making vast amounts of information seem more manageable.

I've spent my lifetime around Carolina basketball, so writing about the Tar Heels was somewhat easy. But I had little background with Kansas hoops. Dave Ranney of the *Lawrence Journal-World* provided research material and also put me in touch with Jerry Waugh, an assistant coach on the 1956–57 Kansas team. Coach Waugh was very forthcoming about reliving a year that, as he said even a half century later, "only bothers me every five or six minutes."

Tom McCarthy at Lyons Press jumped at the idea on the first day it was proposed to him; without him there would be no book. Sarah Mazer has now edited two books on Carolina basketball in the past two years, and her efforts have made both of them significantly better.

This book was largely written while the 2005–06 basketball season was in progress. For that reason the 2006 Tar Heels also played a role in the book even though they may not have realized it. Dewey Burke, Mike Copeland, Bobby Frasor, Marcus Ginyard, Danny Green, Tyler Hansbrough, Wes Miller, David Noel, Will Robinson, Byron Sanders, Reyshawn Terry, Quentin Thomas, Thomas Wilkins, and Surry Wood made the season memorable not because they won a lot—which they did—but because of the team-oriented way they did it. I think even a grizzled old veteran like Frank McGuire would have enjoyed watching them play.

It helps that the team was led by the best coaching staff in college basketball today. Roy Williams—who has enormous demands on his time but still agreed to write the foreword for this book—and assistants Joe Holladay, Steve Robinson, Jerod Haase, and C. B. McGrath have done more than just win two national championships (in 2005 and 2009) since coming back to UNC. They have returned Carolina basketball to all the things that make it special, aside from just a bunch of wins on the court. Eric Hoots belongs in this paragraph as well; the enthusiasm he has for Carolina basketball makes it fun to be around the basketball office.

Lauren Brownlow signed up to be a TarHeelBlue.com mailbag intern and ended up learning more than she ever wanted to know about the 1956–57 basketball season. She was indispensable to the writing process. One day in the not-too-distant future, she'll be writing a book of her own; hopefully she'll let me transcribe an interview or two for her.

Steve Kirschner and Matt Bowers provided their usual excellence from the Carolina sports information department. Steve has been kind enough to allow me the opportunity to essentially live a dream over the past five years. Matt suffered through most of the 2006 road games in the seat beside me and somehow maintained his professionalism despite the fact that I would invariably punch him at key moments.

This is approximately the time when the Oscar telecast producers would start playing the "wrap it up" music in the background. Quickly, here are others who deserve special thanks.

Tar Heel Monthly staff members: Grant Halverson, Bill Cole, Lee Pace, John Stillman, Matt Morgan, Lorie German, and John Kilgo helped keep things running smoothly at my day job.

UNC athletic department: Dick Baddour, Larry Gallo, Beth Miller, J. D. Lyon Jr., Matt Terrell, Clint Gwaltney, Karlton Creech, John Montgomery, John Brunner, Ken Cleary, and Michael Beale all helped in some fashion. Jones Angell and Eric Montross made a season of radio postgame shows immensely fun (and for the most part, we stayed out of trouble).

The teachers: Jeff Jeske, Sandra Umstead, and Jill Whitaker showed me how to write and provided the confidence that it was something worth pursuing.

The travel party: Billy Puryear, Ray Gaskins, Liz Daniel, Rob Bowen, and Jim Staten often made it possible for me to eat breakfast with my family, do an interview in some far-flung location, and still make it home for dinner.

The books: Robert Cherry's *Wilt: Larger Than Life*, Dean Smith's *A Coach's Life*, Frank McGuire's *Offensive Basketball and Defensive Basketball*, Scott Fowler's *North Carolina Tar Heels: Where Have You Gone?*, and Al Featherston's *Tobacco Road* proved to be invaluable resources.

The fans: Carolina basketball fans are what make books like this possible. Were it not for their unflagging devotion to all things Tar Heel, people like me would have to find a real job.

For some reason families always occupy the anchor position in these types of acknowledgments even though they probably deserve to be listed first, middle, and last. My parents, Jim and Dubba Lucas, were instrumental in developing my love of Carolina basketball. And even when they have thought I should be writing about torts rather than sports, they have been consistently and overwhelmingly supportive.

My children, McKay and Asher, don't really understand yet what I do that requires staring at a computer screen all the time. One day I hope that they will understand, and that it will make them 1 percent as proud of their dad as I am of them.

My wife, Stephanie, puts up with too many nights when her husband is at a game or a practice rather than at home. She has grown accustomed to eating dinner during a timeout or halftime or after the postgame show. She has learned that she doesn't know her own life's schedule until the latest football, basketball, or baseball schedule has been released (even then, the routine is subject to change due to the whims of television). Yet she still has somehow found a way to be the best mother and wife I know. Many times sports people try to describe their families in sports terms. But Stephanie is too good for a sports analogy, and as she well knows, that's the highest compliment anyone can receive in our house.

Prologue

So this was the way the dream season would end. In Kansas City, in front of a crowd of strangers who knew little about the North Carolina Tar Heels. No family members, few Carolina fans, and only a handful of media. After 30 straight wins, Frank McGuire's magical ride was finally about to end.

He had piloted his Tar Heels to one of the best seasons in school history. They had survived several potentially season-ending games, including a narrow escape from Wake Forest in the ACC Tournament semifinals. In that game they had needed a late—and controversial—three-point play from superstar Lennie Rosenbluth to advance to the finals and then the NCAA Tournament. Even before that, McGuire had conceded defeat to Maryland during the regular season, gathering his players around him in the huddle with two minutes left and instructing them on how to handle the loss. But they were unwilling to accept defeat and came back to triumph over the Terrapins.

It was becoming apparent, however, that there would be no comeback on March 28, 1957. The Tar Heels were matched against little-known Michigan State in the national semifinals of the NCAA Tournament. The game was widely seen as nothing more than a warm-up for the anticipated championship clash between Carolina and Kansas—but it looked like Carolina wouldn't even make it to the final. The Spartans held a 66–64 lead with less than 10 seconds remaining. Their best player, Johnny Green, was at the free throw line shooting one-and-one. If he made even one shot, the game was over.

As Green toed the line, one of his Michigan State teammates sidled up to Carolina point guard Tommy Kearns. Most of the media contingent had spent the week leading up to the game hyping Carolina's undefeated record. Everyone knew the Tar Heels were 30-0. So as Green released the shot that would certainly wipe out the potential Kansas-Carolina matchup, Kearns wasn't surprised at what the Spartan guard said: "Thirty and one."

Chapter 1

A Basketball Coach for a Football School

The University of North Carolina was a football school in 1952. About this there was no question. It was a decidedly Southern university, and that meant it treated its sports the Southern way: The head football coach had the biggest office; football Saturdays were festive; and the male portion of the student body dressed up in their sharpest ties for the Saturday afternoon kickoffs at 24,000-seat Kenan Stadium, a generously proportioned venue for the era.

The state of North Carolina had just 4.4 million residents; the student population at UNC was approximately 6,000. The first African-American law school student had enrolled in June of 1951, and the first black medical school student followed a few months later. It would be the summer of 1955 before the first three black freshmen would set foot on campus.

Of the 6,000 students, very few were women. Unless they were Chapel Hill residents or enrolled in the nursing program, females were expected to attend the Women's College in Greensboro and transfer to Carolina as juniors.

Most of the school's males had grown up playing football or baseball, not basketball. Basketball was a cult sport, although it did have its admirers. One gangly 6-foot-6 freshman by the name of Thomas Wolfe went out for the team in 1915 but was cut because, at 145 pounds, he was too thin. (No matter; he eventually turned to writing to occupy his time and went on to author *Look Homeward, Angel*, considered one of the greatest coming-of-age novels in the English language.) A mid-1950s UNC athletics handbook rambles on for two pages about football before ever mentioning basketball. According to the handbook, "Prosperity in all phases of the athletic area seems to accompany king football."

Football might have been king, but the kingdom was somewhat barren. The Tar Heels had not had a winning season on the gridiron since 1949. But the shadow of the legendary Charlie Justice, who had led Carolina to the 1948 Sugar Bowl and 1949 Cotton Bowl, still loomed over campus. Justice—better known to his fans as "Choo Choo"—had captured the imagination of the entire region in a way no college sporting figure had ever done before. He passed, ran, and punted the Tar Heels into the collective consciousness of the nation's sporting public and did it all as a real homegrown superstar from Asheville whose speech bore a familiar Southern lilt. He was a two-time Heisman Trophy runner-up, the subject of a Benny Goodman song, and the feature of a *Life* magazine cover. After his Carolina career Justice moved on to the Washington Redskins, still close enough for his Tar Heel fans to follow his exploits.

Basketball had no comparable legend. So it went largely unnoticed when head basketball coach Tom Scott, a native of Pittsburg,

Kansas, resigned in the summer of 1952 after compiling a 100–62 record in six seasons. He was not especially well loved in Chapel Hill and was coming off a pair of consecutive sub-.500 seasons. His team played in 5,000-seat Woollen Gymnasium but rarely filled it; the Heels had not made the Southern Conference Tournament final since Scott's first season, 1946–47. The coach had alienated some of the few basketball diehards early in his career by benching star John "Hook" Dillon. Scott didn't believe Dillon's style of play fit with the Tar Heels. But the player was popular, and letters of complaint rolled into the basketball office.

That was three seasons before the wins started to dry up for North Carolina. But the bad feelings lingered, and they eroded any reserve of goodwill Scott might otherwise have possessed among the fan base. When he was asked to coach the Phillips 66 Oilers, an Amateur Athletic Union (AAU) team that had won the national title in its division 8 of the past 11 seasons, he quickly accepted. Scott called it a "once-in-a-lifetime" job; no one in Chapel Hill begrudged him the opportunity.

There was little speculation about the next head of the North Carolina basketball program. A brief story in the campus newspaper, the *Daily Tar Heel*, mentioned Jim "Pappy" Hamilton, the head coach at Lenoir-Rhyne College, as a possibility. Hamilton had played under Scott at Carolina and coached the UNC junior varsity team before leaving for Lenoir-Rhyne. Earl Ruth, a three-year letterman from Salisbury, was also considered and briefly believed he had gotten the job before the focus of the search turned elsewhere.

Scott resigned in May. Summer arrived and brought with it the humidity native to North Carolina. Still there was no new head basketball coach at UNC.

O

North Carolina State ruled the state basketball landscape in 1952. Wolfpack head coach Everett Case had arrived in 1946 and proceeded to dominate his local rivals, making extensive use of the pipeline of high school talent he had developed in Indiana as a 22-year prep coach. State had walloped Carolina three times during Scott's final season, including a 71–52 thumping in the penultimate game of the season. That represented the 14th straight Wolfpack victory over the Tar Heels, a streak that stretched back to 1947.

Some things were simply accepted as fact within the borders of the state in 1952: Tobacco was the king crop and cash producer, the state would vote Democratic in the next United States presidential election (just as it had in 18 of the last 19 elections), and NC State would whack North Carolina on the basketball court.

So it raised some eyebrows when a fast-talking Irishman named Frank McGuire brought his virtually unknown St. John's squad into Reynolds Coliseum in 1952 and defeated the Wolfpack in the first round of the NCAA Tournament. In the next round McGuire's Redmen defeated Kentucky. In back-to-back games, he had beaten Everett Case and Adolph Rupp, two of the era's coaching giants. In fact, McGuire nearly won the 1952 national championship, taking St. John's all the way to the final game before losing to the Kansas Jayhawks. (It would not be the last time that Kansas—or a little-used reserve named Dean Smith, who played just 37 seconds for the Jayhawks in that title game—intersected with McGuire's career in an important way.)

McGuire seemed like a perfect fit at St. John's. Raised in Manhattan's Greenwich Village, he was the 13th child of a New York City traffic cop. His roots in the city were deep. Even his wife, Pat, had grown up in the Gramercy Park neighborhood. If McGuire could restore the Redmen to the top of the city's basketball world, then he would be a hero in the town he loved.

That possibility didn't stop the UNC administration from wondering if he had any interest in the Carolina head coaching position. Forego the chance to be New York City's basketball don for an opening at an also-ran school in the Southern Conference? At first glance the proposition didn't seem to make much sense.

But McGuire had ties to the area. His stint as the head basketball coach at his prep alma mater, Xavier High School in Brooklyn, had been interrupted by Navy duty during World War II. Part of his service time was spent in Chapel Hill as an officer in the V-5 training program. He befriended Y. Z. Cannon, a local barber, and discovered that the local high school needed some help with its basketball team. McGuire volunteered as a coach during his off-duty hours and began to build a rapport in the insular community of Chapel Hill.

Almost a decade later, he still fondly remembered his time in Carolina. When St. John's played at Reynolds Coliseum in the 1952 NCAA Tournament, McGuire made a casual remark that was picked up by the media: He still had Chapel Hill in his blood, he said, and it was tough to get it out. Tar Heel basketball supporters filed away this comment. Maybe, just maybe, the next time they needed a coach they could pry away this smooth talker who had already shown an ability to do something the current coaching staff couldn't do—beat North Carolina State.

McGuire, the ultimate city boy, liked Chapel Hill. It seemed like a simpler place—a solid place to raise his three children, including a son, Frankie, who had cerebral palsy. There were good doctors in Chapel Hill and Durham, so the move away from New York City's medical hub would not be a major loss. Sure, things moved more slowly and people talked funny, but he thought he could use his city connections to bring a different style of basketball to the South.

That's how North Carolina came to introduce the dapper 42-year-old as its head basketball coach in August 1952, just three months before practice began. He was given a three-year contract at a reported $12,000 per season. Fans loved his coaching credentials but were less enamored of some of his other qualities. He was indisputably a Yankee in an era when *Yankee* still qualified as a bad word in some Southern circles. He spoke with a New York rhythm—he didn't speak of guards, centers, and forwards, but of "gahds, centahs, and fo-wads."

But something about McGuire engendered trust in everyone he met. He had a cozy way of speaking directly to whomever he was addressing, calling the person by name several times in course of a one-on-one conversation. People walked away from talking to him feeling as though they had made a new friend who really cared about them.

He was the new head coach of a school with limited basketball tradition—the crowning moments were a 1924 national title awarded retroactively by the Helms Foundation and a 1946 appearance in the NCAA title game—and without much prospect for improvement. Before the 1952–53 season, one magazine ranked the Tar Heels 278th out of the top 600 NCAA men's basketball teams. McGuire took the long view of his prospects in Chapel Hill: He guessed that with capable recruiting and smart scheduling, he could have the Tar Heels competing for national honors by the 1957–58 season.

He knew that his program would initially be nowhere near the level of college basketball's powerhouses, like the University of Kansas. The Jayhawks were coming off the 1952 national championship. Around that same time the school's sports information director, Don Pierce, saw a photo of a high school track and basketball star. The athlete was from faraway Philadelphia, but Pierce mentioned the photo to basketball coach Forrest "Phog" Allen anyway. Allen committed the name of the player—Wilt Chamberlain—to memory. The head coach was too busy winning games (the Jayhawks would return to the national semifinals, not called the Final Four for many more years, in 1953) to worry about some hyped-up high school kid.

O

With only a couple weeks before school was back in session, McGuire had little time to recruit players for his first Carolina team. But his first task was to complete his staff. Today, North Carolina carries one head coach, three assistant coaches, a basketball operations director, a strength and conditioning coach, a video director, and three secretaries.

McGuire's staff was a little simpler: He was allowed to hire one assistant coach.

The identity of that coach was never in question. James "Buck" Freeman had been McGuire's coach when McGuire was a player at St. John's. Freeman had a solid reputation in New York City basketball circles, having served as head coach of the St. John's "Wonder Five" teams that captivated the city in 1930 and 1931. (In the midst of the Depression, 15,000 fans packed Madison Square Garden to watch them play.) Battles with alcohol had dimmed his coaching star and made him a risky hire as a head coach—he had first moved on to the University of Scranton, then Ithaca College—but McGuire didn't need a head coach. He needed an assistant, and there was no one he trusted more than Buck Freeman.

In some ways they were an odd pair. McGuire was always immaculate; he wore a wardrobe by Brooklyn clothier Abe Stark, whose store sponsored the famous "Hit Sign, Win Suit" placard under the Ebbets Field scoreboard in Brooklyn. McGuire was obsessive about personal neatness and would never be seen in public without a coat and tie. He demanded that his players be clean-shaven and reportedly once chased a top prospect out of his office for not wearing a clean T-shirt. In contrast, Freeman always wore sneakers and was usually clad in sweatpants and an athletic top. McGuire had the uncanny ability to appear to be gliding, even when on the practice floor; Freeman was more herky-jerky and gave off a somewhat harried vibe.

But the pair trusted each other implicitly. And Freeman had the one thing missing from the McGuire arsenal: a terrific strategic knowledge of the game of basketball. For all his reputation, for all his bluster, McGuire was not a great strategist. He knew the game; it was impossible to rise to his level in the profession without an advanced knowledge of hoops concepts. But he was not, at heart, a strategist. He was a motivator, the type of coach who could storm into the locker room and whip his charges into a frenzy with an impassioned speech. He rarely won games with tactics. Instead, he used emotion to produce fantastic effort.

Freeman was a strategist whose life revolved around the game of basketball. He didn't care about fancy dinners, didn't care where the team stayed on the road, didn't care what kind of suit he was wearing. He lived at the gym—not in the metaphoric way we talk about "gym rats" today, but in a very literal sense. When McGuire accepted the job, the back of Woollen Gym—which housed the basketball office and all the Tar Heel home games—included a roughly 200-square-foot apartment. That's where Freeman lived throughout his Carolina coaching career.

"He thought about basketball constantly," recalls 1957 Carolina guard Tommy Kearns. "He thought about the little things—things like the release on a shot, the position of your feet when you're shooting, how to use your hands more effectively. He taught players how to handle defenses and what you look for that would enable you to beat your man. He might pull you aside and say, 'That guy who's guarding you crosses his legs defensively. When he does that, that's when you can beat him and take him to the hoop.' You'd go back out on the court, and that's exactly what would happen. That's what Buck was all about. All those little things that no one else paid attention to."

Such exactness made Freeman the perfect second-in-command to McGuire, who virtually never thought about the little things. The duo would spend hours late at night in McGuire's home on Oakwood Drive in Chapel Hill, moving magnetic pieces around a board marked off in the dimensions of a basketball court. Freeman was always trying new ideas; McGuire was flexible enough to implement them to find out what worked.

Freeman's struggles with alcohol were known but not talked about. After all, it was 1952, not too far removed from the era in which newspaper reporters had ridden a train with the New York Yankees, watched Babe Ruth stagger down the aisle with a woman angrily screaming his name right behind him, and then quietly gone back to their card game. They were sportswriters. What happened off the court was not about sports.

So it wasn't news when Freeman occasionally spent the day of a game at a Chapel Hill watering hole. And it wasn't news when McGuire called players to go pick up their assistant coach and take him home to sober up. On rare occasions Freeman did not show up for games; the team knew that he was probably somewhere sleeping off a hard day. He'd be back when he could. McGuire, who had a fierce sense of loyalty, very seldom spoke of his mentor's problems.

○

McGuire and Freeman possessed the same chemistry on the court that they possessed off it. On the bench the head coach was the intuitive leader of the program. He sat with Freeman on one side and a team manager who was instructed to keep running game notes on the other side. The hand-scribbled notes would be typed by the manager overnight and delivered to the basketball office the next morning.

"[McGuire] was very smart," says Ben Lubin, who filled the manager role at UNC in the mid-1950s. "He knew exactly when to call timeouts. He'd watch the players carefully during a stoppage in play.

If he saw someone put their hands on their hips, he knew they were tired and would take him out immediately. Sometimes in the first half he'd put someone into the game at a strange time. Later, he'd say, 'It's going to be a tight game and we might need him in the second half.' That helped us win a lot of close games."

On the bench there was little outward hint of McGuire's feisty Irish temperament. It was a different era of college coaching, one in which coaches rarely stood up from their seats on the bench. McGuire would sit next to the other Tar Heels, clad in his spotless suit, and watch the action unfold. Only players and his closest friends knew how to detect the slightest hint of agitation: When things got tight or McGuire was displeased, his hands would go straight to his tie. He would grab the knot near the collar and firmly straighten it, as if tightening a noose. That was how players knew to anticipate an explosion in the locker room.

McGuire's language was salty, but he could deliver it in public with a shine that made it look from afar as if he was simply having a casual conversation. Late in a game during the 1955 season, the Tar Heels were down by 12 points with only a minute to play. The outcome no longer in question, McGuire removed all five Carolina players and replaced them with five substitutes. He waited for the action to return to the other end of the court, then instructed someone on the bench to lean up to hide what was about to happen. He rose from his seat, walked down the bench, and crouched in front of all five players. He looked the first player in the eye.

"You're a stupid fuck," he said calmly.

Then he looked the next player in the eye.

"And you're a stupid fuck," he said.

Down the bench he went until he had singled out all five players, describing each in the same unflattering fashion. Point made, he stood back up, straightened his tie, and casually went back to his seat on the bench.

Using that type of language while retaining the respect of players is an art form some coaches never master. McGuire, however, knew exactly how to do it.

While the head coach was dealing with the more instinctive aspects of the game, Freeman would revel in the details. He loved to switch defenses, going from zone to man-to-man and back again during the course of several minutes (most teams picked one specific defense and stayed with it throughout the game). One of Lubin's responsibilities was to track how opponents performed against certain defenses. On his pad he would scribble the time the Tar Heels switched to a new strategy and chart the score for its duration. Postgame, Lubin would return to his dorm room and type the results so that Freeman could take the statistics into account the next time the Tar Heels met that opponent. At the time, this qualified as highly advanced scouting.

Players loved the white-haired Freeman for his single-minded approach to the game. In an era when basketball was not a year-round obsession for even players at the college level, Freeman was obsessed with details. Every shot had to be taken exactly the right way—with the ball making a precise number of revolutions while it was in the air and the player's elbow down, his follow-through perfect. Any failure to adhere to these principles would be met with a solemn shake of the head and Freeman's trademark grumble: "Stupid, stupid."

"He was a funny guy," remembers 1957 Carolina forward Lennie Rosenbluth. "He was all about Xs and Os. When Coach McGuire had to go on recruiting trips, he'd leave Buck in charge of practice. Those were some of our favorite practices. We knew he wouldn't be able to take much of us. If practice started at 7:00, he'd throw us out of the gym by 8:00 because he could only take about an hour of us not doing things exactly the right way."

Time showed that Freeman and McGuire made a very effective duo. But in 1952, all their coaching skills would be of no use if they had no players. And at North Carolina, without the tradition or name recognition of NC State, it was hard to find players. During the 1952–53 season the Tar Heel talent pool was so shallow that a team manager had to suit up for an important game just to give the squad enough players to sit on the bench.

But McGuire's first important recruiting move for North Carolina took place before that manager ever donned the blue-and-white home jersey. In fact, it took place courtesy of St. John's. The school held a testimonial dinner to honor McGuire for piloting his team to the national championship game. Only a few people in attendance knew that McGuire was attending one of his last official functions as head coach: McGuire himself, and close friends Harry and Davey Gotkin. The trio told no one about the impending move—except for a talented high school basketball player who was about to make a choice that would reshape college basketball.

Chapter 2

Underground Railroad

Everett Case was moments away from landing the player who would solidify North Carolina State's stranglehold on Southern Conference basketball supremacy.

The venerable Wolfpack head coach was overseeing what essentially was a tryout—not technically a tryout, because that would have been against the rules—on the NC State campus in the spring of 1952. Approximately 100 boys filled the gymnasium, each desperately trying to impress the venerable Case.

One of the boys was a New York City product named Lennie Rosenbluth. He was the quintessential New York kid who used to sit in the Yankee Stadium bleachers and root for Joe DiMaggio. But he couldn't afford to attend the city's prestigious private schools, which were basketball hot spots in the early 1950s. New York private and public schools were two different worlds that rarely intersected on the basketball court. The best talent was assumed to be in the private school system.

Rosenbluth stayed in the public school system. But a teachers' strike his senior year curtailed the basketball season, leaving him with nowhere to show off for college coaches and their scouts. The lanky Rosenbluth was forced to take the subway to Brooklyn, where he played for the Carlton YMCA, an otherwise all-black team that had won 62 straight games. One of the team's coaches was a New York basketball lifer named Hy Gotkin, who happened to be the cousin of Harry Gotkin, one of the ubiquitous high school basketball scouts that populated the area.

Without mammoth recruiting budgets, college coaches often depended on their connections to those scouts to supply talent. Harry Gotkin was a New York garment manufacturer described by *Sports Illustrated* as "the uncrowned czar of recruiting. [He] sees all and knows all." Gotkin, who was in his early 50s, liked to boast that he usually saw about 300 high school games per year. He would stand in gymnasiums all over the city, hands jammed into the pockets of his brown overcoat, and evaluate players. He had played at St. John's and was believed to have a keen eye for talent; that's why coaches competed to gain his favor.

Like most of his contemporaries, Gotkin had an affinity for one particular school. In his case in the early 1950s, it was NC State. Mike Tynberg, a man so eager to claim a connection to the Tar Heels that he occasionally claimed to be an assistant coach (he later scouted for Marquette, after finding his love for UNC unrequited), was his University of North Carolina equivalent.

Tynberg had no chance at wooing Rosenbluth; the Gotkin connection was too strong. When Rosenbluth asked Harry Gotkin about his college prospects, Gotkin had just one answer: "Go to NC State. It's a great school."

Case had already journeyed to New York to scout Rosenbluth, so it seemed like a logical partnership. "We want you," he told the spindly-legged kid.

Case called in April to arrange a campus visit for the prospect. At least, that's how Rosenbluth understood the situation. Despite playing in the relative obscurity of the public schools and YMCA leagues, he had been a legitimate prospect for several years. As a high school sophomore, he had attended an open tryout for Niagara University held at All Hallows High School. He impressed Niagara head coach John "Taps" Gallagher, who invited him to Buffalo for a campus visit. The visit was a turnoff—a Catholic school that required lights-out at 9:00 p.m., Niagara appeared to Rosenbluth to be "an old monastery in the middle of nowhere"—but Gallagher was undeterred.

Later that winter, he was scheduled to bring the top-20 Purple Eagles to play in Madison Square Garden. He called Rosenbluth to alert him to the visit.

"Look, Niagara wants you," Gallagher said.

"But, Coach, I haven't even graduated from high school yet," Rosenbluth replied.

"That doesn't make a difference," the head coach said. "Come on down to the Garden to watch the game. I'll get you a uniform, and you can sit on the bench. If I can figure out a way to get you in the game, I'll play you."

Rosenbluth declined, but he knew that he was in high demand. And it wasn't just college coaches who wanted him. During the summer of his junior year, he had played in a league in the Catskill Mountains. It was a prestigious assignment, as the league included other talented high school players (among them a gangly center named Wilt Chamberlain), college players, and even a smattering of pros. It bore a passing resemblance to today's Cape Cod League in baseball. Hotels from around the region tried to assemble the best rosters of talent.

(They also gave jobs to the players they sponsored, which explains how Chamberlain became the world's tallest bellboy for one summer during his high school career.)

"That was really where I developed the most," Rosenbluth recalls. "You were playing against all these guys who were so talented, so you had no choice. You had to get better. I developed quite a bit of my game in the Catskill Mountains."

Boston Celtics head coach Red Auerbach, who was moonlighting as a summer league coach, spotted Rosenbluth and offered him the chance to work out with the Celtics. Auerbach believed the sharpshooter had a chance to make the jump straight from high school to the pros. But National Basketball Association officials caught wind of the plan and informed Auerbach that such a crazy idea would never be allowed.

The pro plan was scuttled, but Rosenbluth felt confident enough in his ability that he assumed the trip to Raleigh was a mere formality—maybe check out the dorms, meet a few future teammates, eat well, and sign the scholarship papers. Never the type of player who would practice by himself if a game wasn't available, Rosenbluth had not played competitively in about two months. But it wasn't supposed to matter, because Case had already scouted him and Gotkin had added his seal of approval. Case had even invited Rosenbluth's father to Raleigh for the 1951 Dixie Classic, a regional basketball tournament that pitted Tobacco Road programs against top programs from around the country. The elder Rosenbluth returned with a glowing report on the school and the coach. It seemed simple: His son would travel to Raleigh, work out a little for Case, and become the newest member of the North Carolina State Wolfpack.

"That's what I thought was going to happen," Rosenbluth says. "But when I got down there, I found about 100 kids in the gym. And it was just a tryout. I tried to explain to them that I hadn't played much lately and was out of shape."

The Wolfpack coach told Rosenbluth not to worry about his conditioning, to just run up and down the floor a few times and make his best effort. After heeding this request Rosenbluth was winded but still optimistic. Maybe it really had been a formality.

At the conclusion of the event, Case stopped to talk to Rosenbluth, one of the few New York City products at the tryout.

"Son, we only have one scholarship left," he said, "and we don't want to waste it."

Waste it? Waste it on a player who had excelled against New York City competition? Waste it on a player recommended by Harry Gotkin himself?

The slight was more than just a missed opportunity for NC State to land a talented player; it was the beginning of the end of the relationship between Gotkin and Case. Gotkin's nephew, Davey, had committed to play for the Wolfpack. When he found his minutes limited, it was another chink in the Gotkin/State pipeline.

At the moment, though, Rosenbluth didn't care about soiled relationships or New York pipelines. He needed a place to play college basketball. During the teachers' strike he had worked with a journeyman coach named Buck Freeman to keep his skills sharp. Freeman and Rosenbluth would grab a basketball, find an empty gym, and spend the afternoon tweaking the youngster's shot. His familiarity with Freeman would eventually lead the talented player to a new college choice.

Soon after Rosenbluth returned from his disappointing visit to Raleigh, St. John's honored Frank McGuire for taking the Redmen to the 1952 NCAA championship game. Gotkin had been in close contact with McGuire and was on the verge of switching his scouting allegiances away from the Wolfpack.

"Listen, Lennie, Frank wants you," Gotkin told Rosenbluth. "He wants you bad."

"Well, I don't really want to go to St. John's," the player replied.

"Listen to me," Gotkin said with a conspiratorial whisper. "Nobody knows this yet, but Frank is leaving. He's either going to Alabama or North Carolina, and he wants you to go with him. You're his number-one guy."

Rosenbluth pondered the news, which would not become public knowledge for another three months.

"OK," he said. "I'll go with Coach McGuire."

He didn't know exactly where he would be going. He just knew that he would be playing for Frank McGuire. Alabama and North Carolina were essentially the same place to a kid from New York City—his parents wouldn't be able to watch him play at either school, the people would talk funny, and it would be a long way from home—so he didn't particularly care which school McGuire picked.

The head coach eventually chose Carolina. Unfortunately, his prized recruit could not follow; Rosenbluth's grades were not good enough for immediate admission to UNC. So his mother hocked her fur coat to pay the tuition at Staunton Military Academy in Virginia and sent her son to prep school.

Staunton was just 45 minutes away from Charlottesville and the University of Virginia. Before he packed Rosenbluth off for his new home, McGuire made an impassioned plea.

"I need you, Lennie," he told the player. "I need you to help me build this program."

Those words were important to Rosenbluth. Shortly after his arrival at the military school, he began to hear from Virginia recruiters. Today, such a situation would have required McGuire to make regular trips to Staunton to confirm Rosenbluth's pledge. But over the course of that prep school year, the pair never spoke. Rosenbluth turned away all suitors with one simple phrase: "I'm going with Frank McGuire at Carolina."

Not a braggart, Rosenbluth rarely mentioned his basketball abilities to strangers. When he did, though, whether at home or in Virginia, he invariably received the same response.

Rosenbluth: "I'm going to play basketball at North Carolina."

New acquaintance: "Oh, you mean NC State? Congratulations!"

Rosenbluth: "No, the University of North Carolina."

New acquaintance (looking perplexed): "Where is that?"

His first few games at Carolina might have left him wondering the same thing. Filled with excitement, Rosenbluth arrived early for his first game with the freshman team and pulled on the door to Woollen Gym, one of the nicest facilities he had ever seen. Most of the public school facilities in New York had used wooden backboards. At prep school in Staunton, he had played on a fan-shaped backboard. The mere fact that Woollen had a square glass backboard was extremely impressive to Rosenbluth.

But on this day, he couldn't get in to see that backboard. The door to Woollen was locked, and Carolina's future all-time leading scorer was left rattling the handle in the cold. He eventually gained access 10 minutes before tip-off. The game was played in front of 15 fans.

During the course of Rosenbluth's freshman season (1953–54), the crowds grew. Eventually, as the varsity team stumbled to an 11–10 record, a trend developed: Fans would arrive early for the freshman game to watch Rosenbluth. Then, just in time for the varsity game, they would pack their belongings and leave. The freshman team would play in front of a near-capacity crowd. The varsity usually toiled before a group of approximately 2,000.

O

Rosenbluth was critical to McGuire's success at Carolina. But he represented something equally important—the beginning of McGuire's relationship with Harry Gotkin, which would bring numerous top prospects from New York City to Chapel Hill. Gambling scandals had rocked city basketball in 1951, and allegations of point-shaving at City College of New York prompted many of the city's best athletes to want to play college basketball elsewhere. The major New York colleges at the time were NYU, St. John's, St. Francis, Hofstra, Seton Hall, Fordham, Manhattan, Iona, and Columbia. But they no longer got the pick of the area's best talent. Instead, scouts like Gotkin were cherry-picking top prospects for schools hundreds of miles away.

With the Gotkin-Case relationship dissolved, NC State coaches had to find a new scout to work the area. They turned to Howard Garfinkel, who began his lifetime in basketball by serving as the Wolfpack's New York City liaison.

Garfinkel and Gotkin had endless wars over players, with each accusing the other of improprieties. Today, "improprieties" is a code word for cash, with shoe companies and outlaw schools funneling thousands of dollars to some of the nation's top players. In the early 1950s the extravagance was limited to an occasional ticket to a college game at Madison Square Garden. Scouts didn't have money to distribute— that was obvious by the meager existence they usually maintained. One of their most attractive offers, however, didn't cost a penny. They offered attention to players often starved for it. Many players in New York's toughest neighborhoods were from first-generation American families. Their parents weren't in the stands every night, and they didn't have college recruiters calling on an hourly basis. Scouts made them feel important and occasionally bought them a sandwich at a deli. That qualified as heavy recruiting.

"Look, I just speak to a kid," Gotkin told *Sports Illustrated* later, in 1957. "I talk North Carolina to him. I arrange for the kid to see Carolina's campus at Chapel Hill. I see that he meets some players. Somebody takes him over to Raleigh to see North Carolina State's campus with the railroad running through it. That makes up the kid's mind. He sticks with us."

Gotkin's description of the State campus wasn't bluster. Part of the main line of the Atlantic Coast Line—which would later become the Seaboard System, today's CSX Railroad—bisected the Raleigh grounds. Air-conditioning was just a dream in 1950s-era college dorms, so most students left their windows open to encourage ventilation. That made the bright purple ACL locomotives with their shrill whistles unwelcome guests on the State campus when they made their daily runs.

But before the picturesque Chapel Hill campus—which had no similar railroad problems—could hook a recruit, he had to be persuaded to leave New York City. Most of the players Carolina wooed had only rarely left home. If they flew in for a campus visit, it was probably their first time on an airplane. They would be crossing distinct boundaries between the North and South. The Civil War had ended more than 80 years before, but the two regions remained polarized.

Much of the tension was racial, of course. "Colored Only" facilities were still a reality in most parts of North Carolina. But that was just the most overt difference.

"It was a different world in the South," says legendary sportswriter Frank Deford, who grew up in Baltimore but whose mother was from Richmond. "When you moved down South, you were talking about a completely different group of people. The foods were different: black-eyed peas, grits, things that people from the North never knew existed. Southerners knew the rest of the country looked at them differently, and there was that self-consciousness that came because they felt like everyone else thought they were hillbillies or dopes.

"New York was looked upon as a completely different place, even by those of us in Baltimore. And it's still that way even today. New York is almost alien to everywhere else in America."

McGuire's task was to persuade the natives of that alien land to spend four years of their lives in foreign surroundings. Outsiders often made the mistake of lumping all New Yorkers into one vast group. Insiders, like McGuire, knew the city at large was made up of numerous tiny enclaves separated not by race, but by ethnicity. Neighborhoods of the mid-1950s were still grouped largely by country of origin. This street might be Italian; the next could be Polish. Religion was also a major dividing line. No Catholic had a legitimate chance at the U.S. presidency until John F. Kennedy ran in 1960; throughout the race, his Catholicism was a significant issue for many voters.

One of the common threads that crossed ethnic and religious boundaries was basketball. The best games often weren't the organized contests taking place in high school and college gymnasiums, but the impromptu games in neighborhood parks. That's where up-and-coming high schoolers mixed with current college talent. Players who had made it out of the neighborhoods and earned college scholarships were real-life heroes. In the summer they would return home and play in high-octane pickup games. Today, New York City basketball conjures images of flash, of between-the-legs dribbles and no-look passes. Back then, though, it was a cerebral game centered on fundamentals. The rules were simple: losing team gets off the court. To win, players quickly learned that they had to defend, they had to rebound, and they had to set screens.

Prep players would sit for hours on the sidelines, waiting for a chance to join the action. Many of them had entered into the prep school world via scholarships, for which the competition was extremely intense. Some New York private schools cost up to an astronomical $50 per week, so for many first- and second-generation immigrant families, scholarships were the only way to provide a quality education for their children. Coaches would throw open the doors to the gymnasium and hold open tryouts, with hundreds of kids competing for the right to earn a free education. Given the number of players there, each might get to demonstrate his skills for only 10 or 15 minutes. Playing well in those few minutes could change the life of a teenager—not just because he would get to play a sport in high school, but because the education he received there could springboard him into a different culture.

McGuire provided a firsthand look into that culture. Long before Pat Riley made sharp dress on the sidelines fashionable, McGuire was watching over his teams in silk suits. He would walk into a recruit's home and proceed to win over the father with his stories about cops and robbers and the mother with his charm and manners. He was an Irish Catholic who knew how to use those affiliations in his favor.

McGuire also knew how valuable private school scholarships had been to most of the families he was recruiting. He could offer them a similar advantage: the chance for their sons to continue to play a sport they loved while getting a quality education. Few players in the 1950s viewed basketball as a career; it was simply an extracurricular activity. At Carolina an out-of-state scholarship was worth $1,250. With training table meals included, the value vaulted to $2,000 per year, and players also received $15 per month for laundry and dry cleaning.

○

Such terms were attractive to four New York players—Joe Quigg, Bob Cunningham, Tommy Kearns, and Pete Brennan—who would eventually join Rosenbluth and form the core of a very special team: the undefeated 1957 squad. But before he could think of winning championships, McGuire had to survive some lean years in Chapel Hill. His first Tar Heel team went 17–10 and was eliminated in the quarterfinals of the Southern Conference Tournament. One year later, which marked the birth of the Atlantic Coast Conference, the team finished just 11–10 overall and 5–6 in the league. McGuire might have had an enormous reputation in New York City, but in 1954, his ability to bring the same level of success to Chapel Hill was no certainty.

He got a good start with Joe Quigg, an essential recruit who was the exact opposite of Rosenbluth. Whereas the public school kid was largely unknown in the lucrative talent pools of the New York Catholic leagues, Quigg was one of its best products. He had led his squad to the city championship in his junior season and carried considerable sway with coaches and players in New York. So well respected was Quigg that when a fellow New York prep named Bob Young scored 32 points against him in a head-to-head matchup, it instantly catapulted Young onto Carolina's recruiting radar. Harry Gotkin passed the word to McGuire, and within a few months Young had a scholarship offer from North Carolina, where he, too, would become part of the 1957 championship team.

McGuire's smooth delivery in the living rooms of recruits proved to be irresistible for the Catholic Quigg family. "My parents were worried about me going down to the Protestant South," Quigg says. "At that time the Catholic population of North Carolina was miniscule, and they wanted to make sure there would be a church in Chapel Hill. There was a little church called St. Thomas More, and Coach McGuire promised my mother we would all go to church on Sunday."

In reality such outings rarely happened, but the idea of them was a great selling point in the living rooms of concerned families. Quigg signed on for Carolina. Due to a quirk in his academic calendar, he was eligible to enroll in January of 1954. That proved to be the key to unlocking New York for the University of North Carolina.

"I did end up being kind of like the pied piper for the rest of the guys," Quigg says. "I was down there six months before them, and I spent a lot of time telling them how nice it was. It was a big deal to them to hear that from me, because we had played against each other a lot in the city and they knew I was a New York guy."

The New York–Chapel Hill railroad was beginning to click. Another scout in the Manhattan area was Bill Kennedy, who was enormously loyal to McGuire. Kennedy lived just 5 blocks from All Hallows High School in the Bronx, where Bob Cunningham was a star guard. College offers were pouring in for Cunningham, but he was intrigued by the prospect of playing for McGuire and the chance to feed the ball to Quigg. ("Joe was about 6-foot-8, and he was like Mr. Macho," Cunningham says now. "When he announced that he was going to the University of North Carolina, I figured that was the start of a pretty good team.")

Kennedy, who had never met his target in person, sent word through the All Hallows coach that he wanted to sit down with Cunningham and discuss the possibilities for him at North Carolina.

"I was so thrilled about that," Cunningham recalls. "So my mother went out and bought me a brand new leather jacket. One day after school, I go to Mr. Kennedy's building. It's a walk-up apartment with no elevator. I climb the steps, and I knock on the door. I hear this shuffling, and here comes Mr. Kennedy with these two little schnauzers right behind him.

"I go into the apartment and these dogs are barking like crazy. Mr. Kennedy grabs my jacket and leaves for a minute. When he comes back, we go into the living room. The place is full of newspapers. They're everywhere, all kinds of sports clippings. Mr. Kennedy starts talking to me, and all he can say is how great North Carolina is. He shows me article after article about how great Frank McGuire is.

"Finally, I start to get tired of it. So I tell him a little lie, that I have to go home and study. He goes to get my jacket, and when he brings it back to me, there is a huge hole in the sleeve where the dogs had chewed all the way through it. It was the first time I had ever worn it!

"He was embarrassed, but he didn't have any money. So I had to wear it home that way on the subway. Of course when I get home, I try to hide it from my mother, but she knows something is going on right away. She says, 'Bring that jacket over here!' She was not happy at all. And that almost blew the whole thing right there, because she did not want me to go to North Carolina if this was the kind of thing that was going to happen."

Fortunately, Gotkin didn't have a dog. And the jacket incident turned out to be only a minor hurdle for the Tar Heels. McGuire made a trip to New York to visit Cunningham's home early in the spring of the prospect's senior year. Other coaches had backed off after Cunningham had to get 38 stitches in his arm following a fluke fall through a glass door. McGuire never wavered. He oozed his trademark charm, and the Cunningham family—first-generation Americans who had been raised Irish Catholic—soaked it in.

The head coach was dressed impeccably and said all the right things. He promised to make sure their son went to church. He explained the value of a state university education rather than the private Catholic education the Cunninghams thought they wanted. He drank tea and regaled the family with stories about the "old country." He was one of them, he told them. He had grown up around the corner and knew what it was like to struggle in America.

After two hours, he left. Cunningham's mother gave her seal of approval immediately.

"I like that man, Bobby," she said. "I trust him. You can go play ball with him."

To cement the deal, Cunningham made an official visit to Chapel Hill a few weeks later. A substantial climate difference exists between New York City and Chapel Hill in late March. In North Carolina it's a season full of sunshine and blooming flowers. In New York it's still overcoat weather. Cunningham walked the campus and soaked in the college environment.

"I saw all the trees and all the beautiful coeds, and I couldn't believe it," Cunningham says. "I was so impressed. Everybody kept saying hello to me even though no one had any idea who I was, and you don't get that in the city."

Although Cunningham was in the fold, more backcourt help was needed. The NCAA allowed teams to grant up to 18 scholarships per year. McGuire didn't ignore homegrown talent—he offered scholarships to several North Carolina natives during his early years at UNC. But he simply felt more comfortable coaching New York players. That feeling came through in the recruiting process.

Cunningham was a defensive wizard but not well known as a shooter. Another guard McGuire wanted, Tommy Kearns, was the opposite. Kearns played with a New York City swagger. The Carolina head coach first noticed it in 1952, when he went to scout a Kearns teammate at St. Ann's Academy (which would eventually become legendary basketball powerhouse Archbishop Malloy). Instead, McGuire found himself captivated by a cocky sophomore reserve who played with a certain flair.

The head coach filed away the name of Tommy Kearns. Two years later, despite the fact that the priests at St. Ann's refused to send his transcript to UNC (preferring that he attend St. John's), Kearns joined Cunningham in a rapidly ballooning recruiting class.

The final piece of the class was forward Pete Brennan. He had played against Quigg in grammar school and was impressed when Quigg picked Carolina. Although Brennan had numerous college offers and felt a strong pull to Notre Dame, he chose to visit Chapel Hill. On his visit he was paired with a fellow high school senior from New York, a high-scoring Brooklyn native named Johnny Lee who was also considering Yale.

Both players were entranced by what they saw at Carolina. But on the drive home, the group—which included Lee's mother—passed by a large DuPont plant in Delaware.

"Wow," Johnny Lee said. "I'd like to be in charge of one of those one day."

"Yes," his mother said, "and I bet the man in charge of that one is more likely to be a Yale man than a Carolina man."

Brennan knew immediately that Lee would never be his teammate at North Carolina. A few days later Lee declared for Yale, where he would go on to great success—as indicated on the cover of the January 31, 1957, issue of *Sports Illustrated*.

Despite the comments of Lee's mother, Brennan chose Carolina.

His decision in the spring of 1954 cemented the recruiting class that McGuire hoped would be his foundation at North Carolina. His only problem was that NCAA rules prohibited freshmen from playing with the varsity, so he wouldn't be able to use the New York–laden class as a whole until the 1955–56 season. With the birth of the Atlantic Coast Conference and the ever-present menace in Raleigh, that seemed like a very long time away.

○

Carolina was never a serious contender for the services of Wilt Chamberlain, a product of Overbrook High School in Philadelphia. Like Rosenbluth, Chamberlain had already caught the eye of the NBA, and the league amended its territorial draft in 1955 to include high school players. That enabled the Philadelphia Warriors to procure Chamberlain's draft rights four years before he would otherwise be eligible for the 1959 selection process.

But first he had to attend college. He had led his high school team to a 56–3 record in his three-year career and was one of the most sought-after recruits in basketball history. The recruiting heated up once schools learned that Chamberlain wanted to leave the Philadelphia area; many sports experts had assumed that he would attend school close to home.

Legendary Kansas coach Phog Allen flew to Philadelphia to scout the 7-footer and was immediately smitten. Chamberlain's mother was likewise taken with Allen, and after a campus visit went well, the Jayhawks became the leading competitor for Chamberlain's services. The player would later tell several New York newspapers that another factor in his decision was the promise of cash payments; Chamberlain said he received $4,000 from "two or three godfathers" while playing at Kansas.

Chamberlain's college choice was the subject of a five-page feature story in *Life* magazine. The typically low-key Allen (who also coached Dean Smith, himself destined for a legendary head-coaching career) had a deadpan response when informed that he had secured Chamberlain's commitment: "I hope he comes out for basketball."

O

McGuire relished the attention his New York connections received. The *New York World Telegram* and *New York Sun* both ran a cartoon depicting a Chapel Hill stop on the New York City subway line. The Carolina head coach was delighted—he had two copies framed and hung one in his office and one in his living room.

"New York is my personal territory," he boasted to *Sports Illustrated*. "Duke can scout in Philadelphia and North Carolina State can have the whole country. But if anybody wants to move into New York, they need a passport from me."

Right-hand man Gotkin agreed: "North Carolina owns New York now. None of the kids Frank wants get away because I feed them a good line."

McGuire could get them to Chapel Hill, but he couldn't always make them comfortable there. His first morning on campus, Cunningham stopped by the venerable Carolina Coffee Shop, a campus institution on Franklin Street. He placed a simple order: bacon, eggs, and a cup of coffee. After a pleasant wait, during which he experienced the usual Southern phenomenon of strangers saying hello, his order arrived. Cunningham had just one thought: "What the hell is that stuff?" He called the waiter over to his table and pointed to the creamy white substance on his plate.

"I'm sorry, I didn't order any Cream of Farina," he said, referring to the popular hot breakfast cereal. "I don't want that on my eggs."

The waiter looked perplexed. "What do you mean?" he asked.

"I just want bacon and eggs," said the basketball player, rapidly growing irritated with the failure to communicate. "I didn't order Cream of Farina."

The waiter began to laugh.

"Son, where are you from?" he asked.

Now things were getting personal. Cunningham sat up as tall as his seat would allow. He'd never been called "son" before by anyone who wasn't his father.

"New York City," he said proudly. "Why does it matter?"

The waiter nodded his head as though he had confirmed a suspicion. Then he proceeded to explain to his customer that the mystery substance on his plate was not, in fact, Cream of Farina.

It was grits.

Chapter 3

Tobacco Road Tradition

North Carolina and Duke played a basketball game on March 4, 2006. But by the time powerhouse sports network ESPN finished with it, it was much more than just a simple two-hour game.

The network chose the renewal of college basketball's best rivalry to debut its ESPN Full Circle broadcast approach. The game itself was aired on regular ESPN, with familiar announcer Dick Vitale bringing his unique brand of enthusiasm to the production. For most games Vitale's presence would have been sign enough that this was a big game. This time, though, the loquacious commentator was little more than a small piece in a mind-boggling puzzle.

While ESPN was broadcasting the game, viewers could tune to ESPN2 to watch the entire contest from a special "above the rim" camera mounted over one of the backboards. Simultaneously, ESPNU shot the game from a handheld camera in the Duke student section in an effort to provide viewers with the sensation of being a member of one of college basketball's most publicized student bodies. On the Internet, ESPN360 provided in-depth stats, live chats, and viewer polls to fans via their computers. For those fans who had to leave the house, ESPN Mobile provided constant updates to mobile phones. And the game wasn't just an American phenomenon—ESPN International sent the matchup live to more than 120 countries.

All weekend, ESPN Classic showed famous Carolina-Duke contests of the past. Before the 2006 game ESPN broadcast hours of coverage from Cameron Indoor Stadium for the College GameDay program. After the game ESPNEWS aired the postgame news conferences live. Ninety-nine ESPN employees made the trip to Durham just to help with game production; an additional 50 were in town to assist with the GameDay production.

Students camped out for a month for the right to attend. It was, as usual, a sellout. The game collected a 3.5 rating; approximately 3.78 million households watched it on ESPN and ESPN2. In the moments before the game, one scalper offered a pair of tickets—upstairs in the corner, perhaps the worst seats in Cameron Indoor Stadium—for $500 apiece.

He found an eager buyer.

North Carolina and Duke also played a basketball game on February 4, 1956—50 years and one month to the day before the meeting just described. Carolina was ranked 9th and Duke 10th. Attendance was fewer than 8,000 people. Tickets were marked $2, and no reports of scalping were recorded. Television coverage was nonexistent; radio coverage was spotty. The game did, however, rate a story on page six of the next day's *Daily Tar Heel*. Such coverage was considered fanatical in the mid-1950s.

That was the reality of basketball in the early days of the Atlantic Coast Conference. Frank McGuire had come to North Carolina to coach in the Southern Conference, but that league dissolved after his first season (1952–53). Seven members—Carolina, North Carolina State, Duke, Wake Forest, Maryland, South Carolina, and Clemson—had become unhappy with the league's ban on postseason play, so they drafted a new set of bylaws and withdrew en masse on May 8, 1953. Just over a month later, on June 14, the Atlantic Coast Conference formed. Because a seven-school conference would have had trouble staging a lucrative postseason basketball tournament, Virginia was admitted as the ACC's eighth member on December 4, 1953. Despite playing just five league games that season, the Cavaliers were included in the first postseason tournament in the spring of 1954.

○

NC State dominated many of the early ACC events. The Wolfpack had a few built-in advantages—most notably, the tournament was played in their home arena, Reynolds Coliseum—but they also took the sport of basketball more seriously than many of their competitors. That tradition had begun some years earlier, in the mid-1940s.

Burdened with outdated facilities and less tradition than their neighbors at Duke and Carolina, State had tired of trying to compete for championships on the gridiron. Instead, the school turned its attention to a sport with shallower roots in the region but the potential to grow in popularity. The main college basketball excitement in North Carolina had come when the 1946 Tar Heels advanced to the NCAA championship game, but even that enthusiasm was muted, and Carolina rapidly lost any momentum the performance had engendered.

To be competitive in basketball required fewer players and less money than football. What the Wolfpack needed was a coach who could capture the imagination of the fan base, sell the game to uncertain fans, and—most important—win with great frequency and style.

The university turned to the military. The Navy, to be precise, where a former Indiana high school coach named Everett Case was serving as a lieutenant commander. Case's winning credentials were indisputable. He came with some baggage in the form of questions about the way he attracted top talent, but reporters of that era were not eager to dig into allegations of recruiting impropriety.

Case paid little attention to homegrown talent and instead recruited from the area he knew best: the state of Indiana. Six Hoosier prep products were on his first NC State team, and they compiled a 26–5 record during the 1946–47 season. They played an up-tempo, exciting brand of basketball that soon resulted in their being labeled the "Red Terrors." It was important that Case won, of course. But it was equally important that his basketball teams scored a lot of points, ran the floor at all times, and appeared to have fun doing it. To a region more familiar with basketball as a plodding game of patterns and set plays, fast-breaking NC State was a trendsetter. Case instituted bold new traditions: His teams were the first anywhere to cut down the nets after a championship victory, and he created the first pep band in the South.

The Pack needed the fan excitement. The university had committed to something absurd in order to lure Case—the construction of a 12,400-seat basketball arena on campus in Raleigh. The capacity was double that of any other facility in the immediate area and left some fans and administrators shaking their heads. What possible use could there be for a basketball arena with more than 12,000 seats? Could football scrimmages be held there? Case insisted that his program would justify the expense, and his foresight proved to be correct.

Reynolds Coliseum remained the largest on-campus arena in the area for almost four decades. By the mid-1950s it had become a major source of anxiety for McGuire. He knew that as long as Reynolds boasted the largest number of seats, it would always host the biggest events. That meant his Tar Heels would consistently be at a disadvantage in the prestigious Dixie Classic and the ACC Tournament.

Upon his own hiring in 1952, McGuire believed that Carolina athletic director Chuck Erickson had promised to build a new on-campus arena within five years. When there was little movement on the project, McGuire began to drop regular hints about the unsatisfactory nature of the playing conditions at Woollen. Erickson said the problem was simple: An astronomical $2 million was needed for a new arena, and the department simply didn't have the money. It turned into a self-fulfilling prophecy: Woollen couldn't generate money because of its small capacity. Because it couldn't generate money, the Tar Heels played just 8 out of 32 games at home in the 1956–57 season, only one fewer than they played in Reynolds. And because the Heels didn't play many home games, the program didn't generate much money.

In Raleigh, State had no such money issues. The team already had the right facility and the right coach. The Wolfpack just needed the wins—and those victories came quickly.

O

The first Atlantic Coast Conference basketball season was a scheduling mishmash. Wake Forest played 12 conference games, Carolina 11, Duke 10, Maryland 9, and NC State 8. Who was the champion? No one was quite sure. A tournament was needed.

Fortunately, the new league's members had experience with the Southern Conference event. Once played at Raleigh's tiny Memorial Auditorium, the contest had grown in proportion to the Wolfpack's popularity. The tournament moved first to Duke Indoor Stadium in Durham, then to Reynolds in 1951; in the process, it had become a moneymaker and a fun event for fans.

Other teams had adopted Case's up-tempo style, so the quarterfinals were a chance to see four exciting basketball games in one day. The winner-take-all nature of the tournament (until 1975, only the league champion was allowed to continue to the NCAA Tournament) helped add drama, and the central location encouraged walk-up sales as the first-ever ACC Tournament opened on a Thursday afternoon in 1954.

Wake Forest, Maryland, and Duke captured victories in the first three games. The nightcap happened to be the marquee game: Case and his Wolfpack against McGuire and the Tar Heels. By that point the two coaches had developed a rivalry fueled by either genuine dislike or public relations savvy, depending on whose account you believed. There was certainly some hard-nosed competitiveness. In his first game against the Wolfpack as Tar Heel head coach, McGuire had broken Carolina's lengthy losing streak to State, emerging with a 70–69 victory at Reynolds Coliseum on January 24, 1953. Not content to just win, McGuire made one extra grandiose gesture: He ordered his team to cut down the nets, mocking Case's signature tradition.

Case made him pay for the win, however. His team throttled the Tar Heels 87–66 in a rematch, and one of the ACC's great early rivalries took hold. McGuire was irked that the Wolfpack head coach had stayed in a pressure defense even after the outcome was decided. Newspapers of the day often did not bother to include postgame quotes from coaches, but this was too good an opportunity to ignore.

"[Case] ruined the game by using the press," McGuire said. "It was ridiculous. He could beat us by 25 points without doing it, and he comes over here and tries to beat us by 40. If that's the way he wants to play, I'll fight him right back when we get the boys to compete with him.

"I don't mind losing, but when a team takes advantage of your weak spot, especially when it can win by other means, well, that's not cricket in my book. I thought he was my friend, but I know better now. I just can't wait until the day comes when I can meet him on equal terms. I'll get even with that rascal."

Case sounded a little amused when told of his rival's comments. "Since when did he get to the place where he could coach my ball club?" Case asked. "I'll do anything I please as long as it's within the rules."

The rivalry made for terrific theater, something both coaches realized. Case liked winning, but he was equally adept at promoting the game. Like a wrestling promoter who needs both a good guy and a bad guy, he knew that the Wolfpack would not profit from being the unquestioned ruler of the ACC. Case needed to win—but he wanted to do so by beating interesting opponents. In McGuire he saw that opportunity.

"He'd always say, 'Don't shake hands on the court,'" McGuire would later report. "He wanted us to let the people think we were mad at each other."

Within the coaches' inner circles, those types of comments always created a cloud of uncertainty as to whether the rivalry was real or manufactured. Case and McGuire were known to dine together occasionally, but they were also known to shout at each other from their respective benches.

The feud between the two coaches helped pack Reynolds to a near-sellout for the 1954 UNC–NC State tournament matchup. But instead of the racehorse tempo the crowd expected, McGuire slowed the game to a walk with a packed-in zone defense designed to force State to shoot from the outside. With six minutes left, State tried to protect a 47–43 lead by holding the ball. With no shot clock and no three-point shot, Carolina needed two baskets just to force overtime. First, though, the Heels would have to gain possession.

The slow-down strategy seemed to lull State to sleep. A pair of turnovers allowed the Tar Heels to bring the score to 47–46. The Carolina deficit was still 1 point when Gerry McCabe scored with 11 seconds left.

The Tar Heels had to foul immediately to get the ball back. Carolina's Tony Radovich did exactly that, but he did it with a little too much vigor. His rough takedown of State's Davey Gotkin—the same Gotkin whose lack of playing time would eventually harm the Harry Gotkin/Case relationship—sparked a brawl. Both players landed in a heap on the Reynolds floor. Gotkin jumped to his feet and whipped the ball off Radovich's head. Twelve thousand spectators looked on with delight as both benches emptied; officials helplessly blew their whistles as pandemonium reigned on the court. In the 1950s, on-court fights were not entirely unusual, but this one seemed special. Fans craned their necks to see if Case and McGuire might square off. As entertainment, this certainly beat a football game.

After several minutes, order was restored. Gotkin received a technical foul, Radovich was ejected, and a generation of the region's sports fans was hooked on this madness they called the ACC Tournament. NC State prevailed 52–51 to advance to the semifinals. After the game Case and McGuire did not shake hands, with each blaming the other for the slight. Were they just following Case's public relations strategy, or were they legitimately miffed?

No one knew, and the uncertainty was part of the attractiveness of the rivalry. NC State would go on to win the inaugural event, but the result was almost inconsequential. What mattered most was that fans walked out of Reynolds Coliseum buzzing about basketball. They would be back the next year to root for their favorites. Thousands of tickets had been sold, and the event turned a staggering profit of $72,000 in its first year of existence.

A Tobacco Road sports tradition had been born.

○

Games against the Wolfpack were known to feature an occasional fracas, but no rivalry brought out pure hatred like that between Carolina and Wake Forest. During the 1956–57 season, Wake would relocate to its present home in Winston-Salem. But prior to the move, the school was actually located in Wake Forest, about half an hour from Chapel Hill. Proximity—and, Carolina alums might add, the Demon Deacons' constant sense of inferiority—bred a passionate feud. "The first thing Wake Forest people learn when they go to school as a freshman is that they want to beat Carolina," says Jackie Murdock, a talented guard on the Wake teams of the mid-1950s. "It's not a course at Wake, but it could well be. It's just something that has always been there."

Few ACC fans gave much consideration to the NCAA Tournament. It was just an event played in faraway locations that was tacked onto the end of the regular season. The true measure of a team's success came in how it fared against its closest rivals and, of course, in the conference tournament. Duke, NC State, Carolina, and Wake were all within half an hour of each other. The term *Research Triangle*, today an accepted part of North Carolina geography, had yet to be coined, but players and spectators at all four schools knew that they were part of a close-knit group. They were called the "Big Four," and their rivalries and classic games fueled the early days of the Atlantic Coast Conference.

Wake Forest was the small private school eager to escape from the long shadow of its public school big brothers. In basketball Wake often drew from a talent pool of North Carolina natives. When McGuire began virtually ignoring the Tar Heel State in his recruiting, it prompted numerous players who might otherwise have wanted to go to UNC to attend Wake instead. The implication, at least among Wake supporters, was clear: McGuire thought he was too good to coach North Carolina boys. He didn't think they could compete with those Yankees he liked so much.

During the 1955–56 season, one year after a football game between the rivals had exploded into a stands-emptying brawl, the two teams squared off against each other on the hardwood on multiple occasions. The Deacons toppled fourth-ranked Carolina in the tiny confines of Wake's Gore Gym, where fan seating extended directly to the edge of the sidelines. A favorite ploy of Wake fans was to pull the hair on the legs of opposing players as they attempted to inbound the ball. Officials could do little to stop it; after all, they were busy trying to keep the players from pounding on each other. Visiting players also knew that they had to be careful when running downcourt near the sidelines at Gore. Wake fans were known to occasionally stick their feet out in an effort to trip opponents.

The game of basketball was much less physical in that era than it is today, and any contact was usually whistled for a foul. There was no hand-checking on the perimeter and no leaning on another player in the post. But when a game exploded, it usually turned physical quickly.

In the 1956 rematch at Woollen Gym, Carolina held an insurmountable lead with 10 seconds left. The crowd was jubilant. After an errant shot, as the final seconds began to tick away, Joe Quigg and Wake Forest center Jim Gilley chased the rebound. Gilley swung his body around, Quigg fell to the floor, Bob Cunningham took exception to Gilley's move and started swinging, and the fight was on.

"The next thing I know, the entire Woollen Gym is in bedlam," Cunningham says.

Punches were thrown, the crowd spilled out of the stands and onto the court, and the latest bout in the Wake-Carolina rivalry was pulsing. As usual, there were plenty of Tar Heel football players in the stands. Many of them swarmed into the brawl, but a handful were charged with a more important responsibility—they had to surround Lennie Rosenbluth and make sure he wasn't injured. The basketball players eventually battled their way to the locker room, where they spent several minutes recounting the action to each other. That's when they noticed that their head coach was missing. There was a brief moment of concern—until McGuire arrived, beaming.

"That's the best right hand I've thrown in 20 years!" he told his team, explaining how he had clocked someone as he battled through the crowd. The ACC investigated and pinned much of the responsibility for the fight on Cunningham. The sophomore guard was suspended for the rest of the season and was booed at Wake Forest every time the teams met for the rest of his career.

Carolina and Wake Forest faced each other again in the 1956 ACC Tournament. In just its third year of existence, the event was already a staple on the Tobacco Road landscape.

"When we played Carolina in the conference semifinals, that had to be the hottest ticket of any game I ever played in," Murdock recalls. "The tickets were purple. Over at Wake Forest there were some guys who were trying to draw up fake tickets. It was unreal."

No punches were thrown in the rematch, but Wake Forest prevailed in a 77–56 rout, giving the Deacons a shot to dethrone the mighty Wolfpack in the conference final. Case's teams had a history of flaming out in the NCAA Tournament after dynamite regular seasons; it was the only blot on a resume that otherwise would have qualified his team for inclusion among the nation's elite programs. Some suggested that Case put so much emphasis on the ACC Tournament that his teams lost their edge after winning what they believed was the season's ultimate competition.

The 1956 team was supposed to reverse the record of underachievement. Case had a veteran squad that included four seniors and a junior in the starting lineup. They rolled over Wake Forest 76–64 in the league tournament final. An eventual national showdown with San Francisco—the 1955 champions, who still boasted powerful Bill Russell—seemed inevitable.

The Pack's first-round NCAA Tournament game against Canisius in Madison Square Garden was considered a mere formality. But previously unknown Hank Nowak scored 29 points, and the game eventually went into four overtimes. In the final period Canisius reserve Frank Corcoran threw in a last-second jumper to provide the 79–78 margin of victory and end the second-ranked Wolfpack's season. Even today, the game is still considered one of the 10 greatest upsets in tournament history.

It also happened to be one of NC State's last chances to stake out a national place for its program. The NCAA Tournament was growing in popularity, and to gain notoriety teams had to succeed on the national stage. Case struggled to do that. Soon, he would find his program embroiled in a recruiting scandal. Jackie Moreland, a Louisiana native, originally had signed a letter of intent with Texas A&M but also had committed to Kentucky. He showed up somewhat unexpectedly at NC State in 1956 and immediately landed the program in trouble. The Pack had just finished a one-year probation for holding illegal tryouts when reports of cash gifts to Moreland and scholarship offers to his girlfriend hit the papers. The ramifications were serious: The NCAA leveled State with a five-year probation deemed "the most severe ever assessed" by the athletic association.

An early 1960s gambling scandal would cause State even more problems. By the time Dean Smith took Carolina to three straight Final Fours from 1967 to 1969, State's gateway to becoming one of the NCAA's signature programs had slammed shut.

O

Even as Case was building the Wolfpack's—and by extension, the ACC's—profile in the early- to mid-1950s, the ACC was doing without most of the modern accoutrements taken for granted today. Case was one of the first coaches to pioneer the use of film in scouting opponents. Most of his brethren in the coaching profession didn't believe in film (although McGuire was known to film his team's games to review later in his tiny office). Instead, with the league so tightly compacted geographically, it wasn't unusual for coaches to go to other games and scout opponents personally. Why invest in expensive and unreliable film equipment when every team in the conference would pass within 20 miles of your campus at some point in the season?

Coaches couldn't count on watching opponents on television, as widespread coverage was still several years away. The Tobacco Road Sports Network had approximately 60 radio stations, with Ray Reeve handling play-by-play and Bill Currie providing color. But that was essentially the only way to follow out-of-town games.

So it wasn't unusual for McGuire to pass word to Lennie Rosenbluth through his roommate, team manager Ben Lubin, that McGuire was planning to head out for a night of scouting. The head coach rarely extended the same invitation to other players, but he and Rosenbluth had quickly developed a unique bond. (It carried over to their significant others: The future Pat Rosenbluth regularly sat with Pat McGuire, the coach's wife, under the basket at home games in Woollen Gym.) Although he was just two years older than most of his teammates—thanks to the year at Staunton—Rosenbluth seemed significantly more mature to the younger Tar Heels. It made sense to them that he would prefer to spend an evening at Duke Indoor Stadium scouting a game with the head coach rather than killing time in the dormitory.

In 1955 Rosenbluth, Lubin, and McGuire went to a Wake Forest–Duke game at Gore Gym. Knowing that they would be unwelcome if anyone saw them, they carefully chose a spot near the top of the bleachers. Duke forward Ricky Rosenthal was a friend of the McGuire family; his father owned a jewelry store in Durham and counted McGuire among his closest friends.

As usual, it was a combustible night in Wake Forest. The tension gradually built until a scrum broke out at the end of the game. From his high perch McGuire spotted Rosenthal as the Blue Devil was separated from his team and lost in the throng of Wake Forest supporters.

"I'll meet you at the car, Bennie," McGuire said.

Before Lubin could react, Carolina's head coach was storming down the collapsible bleachers. He grabbed Rosenthal by the shoulder, delivered a fierce look to the Wake Forest fans standing around him, and escorted Rosenthal to the Duke locker room.

"It really wasn't all that unusual," Lubin said recently, remembering the incident with a smile. "That's just what you expected in the ACC in those days."

Chapter 4
Being Rip Kaplinsky

The 1956–57 season officially began with the start of practice on October 15, 1956. For North Carolina, however, it actually had begun more than seven months earlier.

The Tar Heels had breezed through the previous regular season with a 17–4 record, earning a tie for the Atlantic Coast Conference's regular-season championship. Along the way they had captured Frank McGuire's first nationally significant victory with a win over fifth-ranked Alabama on December 14, 1955. The two programs had numerous parallels; like Carolina, Alabama was led by a fast-talking head coach (named Johnny Dee) who was trying to bring basketball prominence to a university more familiar with football.

Dee, who had been hired when an effort to woo Frank McGuire failed, had a ready-made foil within the league: Kentucky's Adolph

Rupp played the Everett Case role in the Southeastern Conference. Dee and Rupp exchanged barbs through the media, and their relationship was generally thought to be frostier—with most of the pepper added out of legitimate spite rather than a desire to gain media attention—than the McGuire-Case rivalry.

Although the Tar Heels had played a mediocre 1954–55 season (with a 10–11 record), there was a buzz about basketball in Chapel Hill. Diehard fans who attended the program's freshman games left raving about the guard combination of Bob Cunningham and Tommy Kearns and about the rebounding prowess of Pete Brennan. Maybe, they thought, when paired with high-scoring Lennie Rosenbluth on the varsity, the team could do the impossible and defeat NC State regularly—perhaps even win the Dixie Classic!

That excitement led to a sold-out Woollen Gym for the December 1955 visit from Alabama. Carolina was ranked 16th in the country, the team's first national ranking under McGuire. The Tide featured 6-foot-8, 220-pound center Jerry Harper, the highest scorer in the program's history and an All-America candidate. The game was considered a measuring stick for North Carolina—not one they had a legitimate chance to win, but an opportunity to see how far they had to go before reaching the nation's elite.

The answer: They had arrived.

The Tar Heels delivered a 99–77 thumping to Alabama. The contrast on the sidelines was stark. Dee yelled at the officials constantly, bounced up and down off the bench, and opened the top button on his shirt while allowing his striped tie to dangle askew. McGuire, as always, sat poised and flawless on the Carolina bench while watching his team pick apart the more highly regarded Crimson Tide.

Even the *New York Times* was in town to cover the game, as reporters had been working a feature piece on Dee that would run later in the week. Covering a game as a sportswriter in 1955 was considerably more complicated than it is today. First, the reporter would have to pound out his game story on a typewriter, usually smoking while writing. The story was light on postgame quotes, heavy on description of the action. After all, most fans hadn't seen the game and needed a basket-by-basket account of what had transpired. Once finished, the copy would go to Western Union, where it would be filed to the hometown newspaper.

North Carolina sports information director Jake Wade made a habit of walking up and down press row while writers were finishing their stories. He liked to see what was being written about his team before it hit the papers, and reporters usually were too busy to object. The night of the Alabama game, Wade returned to the small sports information office with some head-shaking news.

"The guy from the *Times* wrote a lead that said, 'Mark down North Carolina as next year's NCAA champions,'" Wade told his student assistant, Buzz Merritt, in amazement. The story went on to extol the virtues of McGuire's coaching and the potential of a 1956–57 Carolina team that would feature one senior and four juniors.

The Tar Heels were considered to be one year away from national prominence, but the players believed that they might be able to arrive one year early. They opened the 1955–56 season with seven straight wins before absorbing a 22-point waxing from NC State in the Dixie Classic championship game, which matched the fourth-ranked Tar Heels against the third-ranked Wolfpack. It was one of the most highly anticipated contests in the history of the event.

Carolina got revenge for the loss with a 4-point victory over State in Woollen Gym on January 18, 1956, but lost the rematch 79–73 in Raleigh on February 21. The only resolution was clear: a meeting in Raleigh for the ACC Tournament championship. The Wolfpack earned the top seed in the event; Carolina was seeded second. That left the Tar Heels facing an 18–8 Wake Forest squad in the ACC semifinals on March 2.

This was the game that would launch the 1957 championship season. But not for the reason most Tar Heel fans—or the *New York Times*—expected. Third-seeded Wake blew out to a 37–24 halftime lead and coasted to a 77–56 victory. Rosenbluth made just 10 of 28 shots while Jerry Vayda struggled to a 1-for-11 performance. Brennan played 20 minutes off the bench and missed all seven of his field goal attempts. Tony Radovich replaced Cunningham, who was suspended for his part in the earlier melee, and went just 1 for 9 from the field.

"I really think we had a stronger team than Wake Forest [the teams split in the regular season], but they had a fabulous game," Brennan says. "We were a run-and-shoot type team, and they just didn't make any mistakes. It was clear they were going to beat us badly. McGuire took us out with about one minute to play so that we had to watch the final minute from the bench. I think he wanted to embarrass us, because he knew that by taking us out, the final score would be even worse.

"He wanted us to be embarrassed, and it worked. We went away that summer and worked that much harder. When we got back to school that next fall, we didn't wait until the beginning of basketball practice to get in shape. We were already in shape. We wanted to show that the way the previous season ended had been a fluke."

O

Basketball practice began on October 15, 1956. The news rated a tiny back-page story in that day's *Daily Tar Heel*. Buck Freeman ran a freshman practice at 3:30 p.m. that drew 45 participants. Interest in basketball at North Carolina was growing, and the roster would have to be trimmed by two-thirds within 10 days. The varsity workout began at 7:30 in Woollen Gym, with the squad continuing to practice at night until its preseason game against the McCrary Eagles—an AAU team similar to the Phillips 66 Oilers, who had spirited away Tom Scott—on December 1 in Asheboro.

McGuire had sent each player a letter six weeks before the start of the season outlining what was expected of the team. The letters showed the coach's usual personal touch and were tailored to each individual, but they also contained some period-specific instructions that might seem quaint today: McGuire preferred that his players not participate in pickup games prior to the start of practice. Instead, he wanted them to work on individual skills like shooting or dribbling and perhaps incorporate some light calisthenics such as rope skipping or shadow boxing. Heavy weight training was, of course, not a consideration. The head coach was, however, a proponent of medicine ball drills, which he believed helped loosen the fingers and strengthen the wrists.

Modern-day North Carolina basketball practices are held in the 22,000-seat Smith Center. (The Tar Heels have an additional full-court practice facility at their disposal, but they use it only on the rare occasions when a concert displaces them from their normal home in the bigger venue.) The first 15 rows of seats are pushed back to create an even larger practice setting. Players can do drills or hone their shooting on any of the eight goals located around the perimeter of the arena. Signs are posted throughout the concourse informing passersby that a Carolina basketball practice is in session, and for that reason, the entire floor level and concourse of the arena are closed. Anyone who obtains special dispensation through the basketball office to attend a practice is asked to sit in a designated section of the arena for the duration of practice. One of the team's handful of managers makes the rounds before practice begins to write down the names of attendees.

Frank McGuire did not know the names of the people observing his practices at North Carolina. He didn't have time. He was too busy trying to make sure his team could squeeze in a practice around the various other events taking place in Woollen. If the Tar Heels met during the day, they would have to compete for space with intramurals. McGuire eventually located a huge curtain that could be pulled around the section of the court that he was using. The curtain wasn't for privacy; it was to prevent errant volleyballs and basketballs from other courts from interfering with his team's preparation.

The night practice sessions he implemented before the start of the 1957 season weren't a form of punishment or an ingenious way to prepare his players for the multitude of night games they would have during the season. They simply allowed the team some uninterrupted time in the gym, free from the distractions of other sports.

Practicing at night allowed McGuire to run the kind of practice he loved. He would arrive on the court a few minutes early and dispense one-on-one instruction to any players that happened to already be on the floor. He knew that his reserves would not receive equal minutes to his starters, but he wanted to at least try to make them feel like equal members of the team. Early practices were light by McGuire's standards. He believed that players should be eased into game condition rather than taxed at the first practice. His standard practice philosophies were simple: Follow a difficult drill with a more fun drill, spend no more than 10 minutes on any fundamental, and give a 10-minute midpractice break.

A representative plan from the first week of practice:

7:30 p.m.: Practice begins with a game warm-up
drill
7:40 p.m.: Passing, screening, discussion, and drills
7:55 p.m.: Shooting techniques and areas (discussion
and demonstration)
8:10 p.m.: Shooting drills (alternate running and
standing)
8:30 p.m.: Defensive work
9:00 p.m.: Offensive formation and plays. Discussion
and demonstration of the basic style.
Position requirements, screening, passing,
and shooting possibilities
9:10 p.m.: Dismissal

In Lawrence, Kansas, expectations were high. In his first game as a Jayhawk, on November 18, 1955, Chamberlain scored 42 points and grabbed 29 rebounds in leading the Kansas freshman team to an 81–71 victory over the varsity, the first time in the program's history that the rookies had beaten the veterans. Phog Allen, who had so impressed the Chamberlain family during the recruiting process, by state law had been forced to retire at age 70, but a capable assistant named Dick Harp had replaced him.

The new coach didn't possess the same instant credibility as his legendary predecessor, and he was handed a strong-willed superstar.

"Wilt was politely disobedient," recalls Jerry Waugh, an assistant on the 1957 Kansas team. "He was a prodigy long before his time. He was well beyond his years physically, but he still had so much he could learn. Most people learn to accept that they have to be patient with change. Wilt could not be patient with change because he had so much pride in being able to do something well. He had taught himself to shoot the ball, and he had pride in that. That could make him difficult to coach."

Kansas fans didn't believe any coaching would be necessary. They would simply roll the balls out, watch Wilt score and rebound, and take home the championship. Several college rules had been tweaked for the 1956–57 season, and many believed that the changes had a direct relationship to Chamberlain's unique talents. Reaching above the cylinder of the rim to tip in a basket, now known as offensive goaltending, was outlawed. The feet of a player shooting a free throw were now forbidden from crossing the vertical plane of the charity stripe until the ball hit the backboard or rim; apparently, there was some concern that Chamberlain might try to jump and dunk his free throw. In most cases this would have been a ludicrous consideration, but for the big man anything seemed possible.

"The first thing I noticed about him on the practice floor was his overall strength," Waugh says. "The physical presence of this guy was dramatic. Even in today's game he still would have that kind of imposing stature. He was much more slender than he's remembered as a pro, but he was already a weightlifter in his college days. He worked at staying strong. And for a 7-foot guy, he was a great jumper. In those days, when we saw a tall player, he usually was awkward and unable to get off the floor. That wasn't Wilt. Wilt had the ability not only to jump, but also to run up and down the floor. You rarely saw him get tired."

Chamberlain was joined in the starting lineup by Gene Elstun, John Parker, Lew Johnson, and Maurice King. Many of the voters who anointed the Jayhawks the preseason number one team in the country, however, probably could not name these four men. They knew only one name, and that one name was enough to hand over the top ranking: Wilt.

O

Although he didn't have anyone on his team as well known as Chamberlain, Frank McGuire was facing a similar problem in Chapel Hill. He had recruited a virtual New York City all-star team to Chapel Hill, which meant he had plenty of talent. But he also had a whole team full of players used to being the main offensive scoring option. Brennan and Kearns were especially offensive-minded, but McGuire knew that he would have to persuade them that the team would be better served with Rosenbluth as the offensive centerpiece.

McGuire dismissed Bob Young and Frank Goodwin from the team for disciplinary reasons. Those losses were expected, and the head coach planned to stay in touch with Young, a 6-foot-6 center, just in case he needed to shore up his team's depth later in the season. Rosters had a tendency to be fluid in that era, and McGuire already knew that Tony Radovich would exhaust his eligibility at the end of December 1956. The roster took another hit when Harvey Salz, who had been one of the stars of the 1956 freshman team that lost just two games, was ruled ineligible for the season due to academic performance.

"With Salz in there, the defense couldn't have collapsed around Rosenbluth so often," McGuire said during the preseason. "Harvey could have torn a defense that concentrated on Rosenbluth to pieces with his outside shooting."

Not all the surprises were unpleasant. Seven-foot Billy Hathaway was the team's most improved player in early workouts. Most observers assumed that Joe Quigg, who had averaged 12 points and 9 rebounds per game as a sophomore, was the obvious candidate to start at center. McGuire wasn't so sure. He liked Hathaway's unusual height and also knew that Quigg was one of the few players on the team with an ego that could handle coming off the bench.

Other egos were more fragile. Kearns had seriously considered transferring during a sophomore season that saw him average just 6 points per game, a meager output for the former New York City star.

"I should have been a better player as a sophomore, but I got down on myself," Kearns says now. "I let Coach get down on me, and that created some negative vibes about me and Chapel Hill. At the end of practice one time, Coach McGuire told me he really needed two basketballs: one for me and one for the other four guys. Looking back, he was probably right."

That wasn't an unusual sentiment from the Carolina head coach. In November 1956, at an early preseason practice, he emptied a bag of basketballs and fired four of them onto the Woollen Gym court.

"There you go, guys," he shouted. "You guys won't play together. Each of you wants your own ball, so here they are. You don't want to pass it to each other, so let's see how we do with everyone playing with his own basketball."

Other than the occasional dare from the coach, very little practice time was devoted to offense. Endless hours were spent trying to persuade the entire roster to play the kind of sticky defense that McGuire believed won championships. He would wait until his team had run for hours, tongues wagging, and then initiate the final drill of the day. Standing at the foul line with a basketball in hand, McGuire would divide his team into two squads of five players each, labeling one the offense and the other defense. Then he would fire the ball at the basket, clanking it off the rim every time. The defense had one solemn job: get the rebound. Any offensive rebound was likely to provoke one of the legendary McGuire explosions and cause him to add several more minutes to practice time.

Boxing out was supposed to be automatic for anyone who wanted to earn playing time for North Carolina. McGuire would make sure of it. His team might not be made up of the highest leapers, sweetest shooters, or fanciest passers. But he wanted a team cut in his own image—a team that would dive on the floor for every loose ball, box out as though they earned points for it, and value the basketball.

"We concentrate on controlling the ball above everything else," McGuire said. "We cherish the ball. We treat it like a gold piece. We take only the good shots and try to teach every boy to know his good shot. Controlling the ball is not freezing it. It's maneuvering for the right opportunity."

Everyone on the team realized that a good shot for Lennie Rosenbluth was different from a good shot for anyone else. Rosenbluth entered his senior season already holding numerous school records: most points scored in a game, most field goals in a game, and most free throw attempts in a game. He had school season records for most points, best scoring average, best field goal percentage, and most field goals. He wasn't as physically imposing as Wilt Chamberlain. But he was just as central to his team's offensive attack.

Defense was a different matter. Although McGuire constantly preached the value of defense, his superstar's abilities without the basketball were questionable. McGuire, the tough Irishman, liked his teams to play a physical brand of defense. To play for the Tar Heels—and the coach liked a short bench, so earning appreciable playing time usually meant finding a spot in the starting five—meant understanding one simple rule: no three-point plays were allowed.

"If anyone ever got a three-point play against you, you knew you were out of there," Bob Young recalls. "If you were going to foul a guy, you never let him make the basket. That's how tough we were defensively."

Rosenbluth had spent his career focusing almost exclusively on offense. It showed on the practice floor, where his teammates often knew they would get a quick breather as soon as McGuire became fed up with his star's defensive indifference. Inevitably, as they scrimmaged, they would hear McGuire's shrill whistle.

"Lennie, how many times have I got to tell you?" he would bark while sticking out his knee as if to trip an imaginary offensive player. "You don't play defense like this."

But that was one of Rosenbluth's defensive trademarks. Rather than move his feet to get in position in front of his man, he would stick a slender leg in the opponent's path. It infuriated McGuire, but in a different way than some of his other players infuriated him. After all, Rosenbluth was his scouting companion.

"Lennie was a good athlete," Cunningham says. "If he wanted to make the effort to do it the way Frank wanted him to do it, he could have. But I think he did it just to crack us up. He was on a different level with Frank than we were, in my opinion. Because of Lennie's background and maturity, he wasn't as naïve about Frank as the rest of us. Lennie knew when Frank was just telling another story. When Frank said something to me, I believed everything he was telling me."

To Cunningham, believing everything meant buying wholeheartedly into the legend of Rip Kaplinsky. Despite never playing for the Tar Heels, Kaplinsky was one of the heroes of the Carolina practice floor. Any defensive lapse or missed assignment was cause to invoke the name of the great Kaplinsky, who had played for St. John's in the mid-1930s. Any mention of Kaplinsky was usually paired with similar praise for Hy Gotkin.

"Those two fellows played with me at St. John's," McGuire would tell his team. "They were killers! This is how good they were: When they really wanted to play defense, you couldn't get the ball up the court. They were too tough. Nothing like you guys. You guys aren't killers like them. If I had Rip Kaplinsky on this team, I'd show you some defense. I want you guys to start playing some defense like him."

"I could see these guys in my sleep," Cunningham remembers. "All I wanted was to be able to play defense like this Rip Kaplinsky guy. I would have nightmares over [Kaplinsky and Gotkin], just thinking about trying to do what they could do defensively. Kaplinsky was a giant to me."

Twenty years later, McGuire was inducted into the Brooklyn Hall of Fame, a major honor in New York. Cunningham attended the ceremony and the cocktail party beforehand, a schmooze-fest with the biggest New York City sports names in attendance. Across the crowded room Cunningham spotted McGuire standing in a circle of friends. He went over, greeted his coach, and was received warmly.

"Bobby, let me introduce you to some people," McGuire said.

There were legendary players, coaching luminaries, and the usual assortment of hangers-on. And then McGuire said something that stopped Cunningham cold.

"And this is Rip Kaplinsky."

"I absolutely couldn't believe it," Cunningham says. "I looked down—literally, I looked down—to a man who hits me about my belt buckle. This guy had a bald head, a big cigar sticking out of his mouth, and he's got a big paunch on him. It's just a little Jewish guy! He puts his hand out to shake my hand and says, 'Hi, Bobby. I'm Rip.'"

Cunningham looked at Kaplinsky. Finally in the presence of the demonic defender who had tormented his dreams for so long, he could say only one thing to McGuire: "Coach, you've got to be shitting me. This can't be Rip Kaplinsky."

"Poor Rip didn't know what I was talking about," Cunningham says. "But Frank knew. And Frank broke out in the biggest laughter you've ever heard."

What Cunningham didn't know was that he would later become a new generation's Rip Kaplinsky. When McGuire moved on to coach South Carolina, his guards were the hard-nosed tandem of John Roche and Bobby Cremins. Visitors to the Gamecock practice court would often hear McGuire admonishing his guards with a familiar refrain.

"I had two fellows with me when I coached at North Carolina," McGuire would say. "They were killers! This is how good they were: When they really wanted to play defense, you couldn't get the ball up the court. They were too tough. Nothing like you guys. You guys aren't killers like them. If I had Bobby Cunningham and Tommy Kearns on this team, I'd show you some defense. I want you guys to start playing some defense like them."

In November of 1956, however, Cunningham and Kearns hadn't yet earned Kaplinsky status. Because of ploys like the Kaplinsky plan, it was easy to pigeonhole McGuire as nothing but a motivational coach who spent little time on the details of the game. In reality, when combined with Freeman, he was one of the true innovators of the sport.

McGuire liked to use at least part of every practice for a segment he called "practicing with the clock."

"You have to remember that every other coach you ever played for, all you ever did was scrimmage," says Rosenbluth. "What McGuire was doing was really advanced for that time. He would really break down every part of the game, and we spent so much time on the last two or three minutes."

McGuire was so far ahead of his time that similar tactics were still considered innovative when Dean Smith used them years later. McGuire would put three minutes on the clock and turn to face his team.

"OK, you're down by 5," he would say. "What do you do?" Then he would blow his whistle and watch the first team try to wrestle the lead away from the second team. Certain rules had to be followed at all times. In the case of a loose ball, no one was to try and dribble it while picking it up. These were the final precious minutes of the game; both teams would be swarming to the ball, and a dribble was likely to be swiped away. Instead, McGuire wanted his players to scoop up the ball and hold it.

"Grab it, hold it, and pass it out," he would say.

Because there was no shot clock, a team with the ball and the lead in the closing minutes had an enormous advantage. As soon as the Tar Heels finished practicing one situation, McGuire would reset the clock to one minute.

"You've got a 4-point lead," he'd say. "What do you do?"

While his team was probing the defense, swinging the ball from side to side, McGuire was constantly talking, constantly instructing.

"Two points don't mean anything!" he said if someone attempted an ill-advised shot. "They'll just come right back and score. We want to work it around, make them foul us. It's a lot easier to make a foul shot than a jump shot from 15 feet. Why would you take a jump shot? You don't have to do that. We have the clock and we have the lead. Take some time off the clock, work it around."

The endless drills could be mind-numbing. Day after day McGuire would put his players through the same situations. Sometimes they would practice comebacks, sometimes holding a lead. Always, there was some sort of game situation to be practiced.

Yes, those endless practice days could be boring. But the head coach was teaching his team a lesson. Even when he gave the second team a substantial advantage—something seemingly insurmountable, like a 5-point lead with two minutes to go—his first team began to notice that the other squad rarely executed flawlessly. With the right amount of pressure and savvy, they would turn the ball over or miss a foul shot. Patient, fundamental basketball was almost always rewarded.

"By the time the games started, we felt like we owned the last two minutes of a game," Rosenbluth says. "We're behind? So what? We're behind in practice every day. We knew the other team would make a mistake, and we knew exactly what we wanted to do. We never had a situation where we had to call a timeout and draw up a play out of thin air. We knew it before the game even started. If we were down by 2, we'd do something we'd practiced many times before. If we were up by 2, we'd do something else we had practiced many times before. There were no surprises at all. We knew everything about those late-game situations, from the way we wanted to space the floor to how we wanted to create a shot."

The varsity put those plans into action against the freshman team in scrimmage on November 15, the same day that Elvis Presley's first film, *Love Me Tender*, debuted in New York City. But the touted upper-classmen struggled, mustering just a 62–56 victory. The *Daily Tar Heel* said the supposedly powerful varsity "didn't look any too impressive."

In many ways it was exactly what McGuire wanted. He held another scrimmage two weeks later, just days before his team opened the season. The freshmen jumped to an early 7-point lead after eight minutes, but the varsity rebounded for a 46–29 halftime lead. They eventually cruised to an easy 96–59 win.

It wasn't the 37-point intrasquad victory that raised the most eyebrows. It wasn't Lennie Rosenbluth's 15 points or Tony Radovich coming off the bench to score 14. It was the attendance. This was a lightly promoted game held just a week after Thanksgiving, with much of the campus ostensibly still licking its wounds from another disappointing football season—the Tar Heels had capped a 2–7–1 campaign in Jim Tatum's first season as coach with a 21–6 loss to Duke. Yet 3,000 people turned out at Woollen Gym for an 8:00 p.m. tip-off.

Just two years earlier, thousands had turned out to watch Rosenbluth play for the Carolina freshman team and then stampeded out of the building when the varsity took the floor. Now thousands were turning out for a meaningless exhibition.

There was a palpable buzz about basketball in Chapel Hill. Soon after the last intrasquad scrimmage, the 1956–57 media guide was released. It listed McGuire's home address on Oakwood Drive in Chapel Hill and was all of 30 pages long; 6 of those pages were shared with swimming and wrestling.

○

There was a knock on the door of a Carolina dorm room. The occupying student, probably engrossed in a textbook or working up the nerve to use the hallway phone to call a pretty young coed in his English class, swung the door wide open.

And there stood his local Marlboro cigarettes representative: Joe Quigg.

The basketball star spent his junior and senior years trying to spread the tobacco gospel to his classmates. The job didn't seem particularly odd at the time—after all, Quigg was a smoker, as were several of his teammates. Philip Morris had created a menthol cigarette called Spud that was available in mini-packs of four cigarettes, and it was Quigg's job to go door-to-door hawking the new brand.

"They paid $50 a month, which was completely unheard of," Quigg says. "I was in heaven with that much money. I went to talk to Coach McGuire about it, and he said it was fine."

Although the job gave Quigg some spending money, it also had a downside. In 1956 Philip Morris was riding one of the most successful advertising slogans of its day: Johnny Roventini's particular delivery of "Call for Phil-ip Mor-ris," which instantly made the 4-foot-tall spokesman an American celebrity. Roventini took his famous slogan to radio programs across the country, sat in Marlene Dietrich's lap, shared dinner with Dwight Eisenhower, and sat ringside with Jack Dempsey. He went nationwide when Philip Morris signed on as a primary sponsor of the *I Love Lucy* television show, a slot the company held from 1951 to 1955.

Roventini also made a pilgrimage to Chapel Hill, where he spent some time with a somewhat less illustrious fellow—Quigg. While Roventini might have been a big celebrity in New York, he didn't quite have the same stature in Chapel Hill. Likewise, basketball players weren't yet status symbols just by virtue of being basketball players. So when Quigg took Roventini to Y Court, the central hangout on campus at the foot of the South Building steps, he wasn't exactly thrilled to be spotted with a 4-foot-tall man wearing a red suit and bellman's cap.

"I'm trying to be a big man on campus," Quigg recalls. "I was embarrassed just to be there, just to have to go to Y Court, the big social place of the whole campus, with this little guy. My face was turning red as soon as we walked in. Classes had just changed, so the place was full and there were all kinds of girls around. And all of a sudden he lets out the loudest call you've ever heard: 'Call for Phil-ip Morr-isssss!'"

McGuire's prized recruit from New York City, a major player on one of the most successful basketball teams in school history, had just one thought: "I'm never going to live this down."

But he did live it down, in part because the part-time job made Quigg one of the few basketball players with any spending money.

Very few of his teammates even had a car. When Bob Cunningham learned that sports information assistant Buzz Merritt had a car, he instantly latched onto him. It wasn't unusual for Merritt to hear Cunningham's voice outside his Cobb Dormitory window.

"Hey, Buzz!" Cunningham would yell. "Borrow your car?"

Merritt would toss the keys to his 1951 Ford, for which he had paid $425, out the window, no questions asked. Cunningham would return the car later.

Players didn't always have to leave campus to find something to do. Rosenbluth, who already stood apart on the practice court, primarily kept to himself off it because he was older and also had a steady girlfriend. He met the future Mrs. Rosenbluth at a popular student hangout: the Goody Shop.

Located on Franklin Street near the Carolina Theater, the Goody Shop could be many things to many people. To most students it was a place to grab a soda and a hamburger. To basketball players it was also something else: a place they could drink beer without fear of repercussion. The proprietor, Spiro Dorton, was a close friend of McGuire. The head coach had a simple rule that his players could recite by heart: If you're going to drink beer, don't drink it in town. He'd send them off for breaks with one last admonition: "I don't want any phone calls from people saying I saw you boys uptown drinking beer."

But his players were constrained by their lack of transportation. That's how they found their way to the Goody Shop, where the private back room allowed them to drink in peace. It was also a place with no strict payment schedule. Dorton was legendarily generous with tabs, especially for athletes, politicians, and other public figures. If a player ordered a hamburger and Coke but didn't have enough money to pay for them, Dorton's response was almost always the same: "OK, just sign the chit and pay me when you can."

The Goody Shop was almost a culture unto itself. Regulars knew each other and interacted appropriately. Dorton kept an eye on newcomers, making sure no one was there to bother any of his more well-known clients. To a legion of Carolina students, he was a friend, father figure, and occasional matchmaker (in fact, Dorton was the one who first told Rosenbluth to call his future wife, Pat). The store had a culture all its own. A waiter named Bozo was a longtime fixture; Spiro's father, Pete Dorton, was also a regular behind the counter.

On one occasion, Pete Dorton was manning the grill and the cash register. Pete Brennan stopped by for breakfast, chatted with Bozo, and then went to the register to pay his bill. Dorton was working the grill while smoking a fat black cigar; ash was dripping down his chest.

"Mr. Dorton," Brennan said, "those scrambled eggs were really good this morning. But I think you may have put too much . . ."

At exactly that moment, a heap of ash fell off Dorton's cigar and onto the table in front of him. It distracted Brennan.

" . . . ashes on them," he finished. "Uh, I mean pepper. Too much pepper on them."

Pete Dorton just laughed.

Bozo was black, which made him one of the few African Americans with whom Carolina students regularly interacted. Segregation was uncomfortable for many of the athletes who had grown up on the playgrounds of New York, scrimmaging against people of all colors. (The Atlantic Coast Conference wouldn't see a black basketball player at a member school until Billy Jones Jr. played for Maryland during the 1964–65 season. Charles Scott would become Carolina's first black scholarship athlete when he joined the freshman team in 1966; he played for the varsity during the 1967–68 campaign.)

Wilt Chamberlain had supposedly picked a more racially enlightened school when he signed on with the University of Kansas. But while his future opponents at North Carolina were hanging out with Bozo at the Goody Shop, Chamberlain was finding things more separate than he expected in Lawrence. With a population of 25,000, Lawrence was bigger than Chapel Hill, but not necessarily more progressive.

Chamberlain was embraced as a basketball player. He hosted a 30-minute weekly radio show called "Flippin' with the Dipper" with a young broadcaster named Max Falkenstein on Topeka's WREN-AM. Chamberlain drove to Topeka every Saturday morning to cohost the show, which played the most popular songs of the week. But Dick Harp feared that the show might somehow violate NCAA regulations, so he asked Chamberlain to stop after just six weeks. (Chamberlain's brief radio career ended, but Falkenstein's was just beginning—he was the radio voice of Kansas sports for more than 50 years before retiring after the 2006 season.)

Though they were happy to tune him in on the radio, Kansas citizens weren't always eager to interact with Chamberlain in other ways. It was a curious kind of selective segregation. On one occasion, Chamberlain went to a Lawrence restaurant with Mitt Allen, Phog's son. The owner of the cafe was blunt: "Mr. Allen, we're not going to serve him," he said.

Allen, a lawyer, was not impressed. "If you don't serve him, I'm going to shut this place down," he replied.

The restaurant complied—for Chamberlain. Other African Americans in Lawrence found that they still were not welcome. The scene was repeated at numerous Kansas institutions, including the Dine-a-Mite restaurant, which essentially served as the Lawrence version of the Goody Shop. Black patrons who walked in with Chamberlain were often served without question; if they tried the same tactic without the well-known basketball star, they were turned away.

In the pre-Chamberlain era, the basketball team ate lunch at the Kansas Union on home game days. Coaches then told the African-American players to go back to their dorms and take a nap, which they did without question. Later they would meet back at a small cafe near the arena for pregame Ovaltine and celery. It wasn't until many years later that LeVanness Squires, the first black player in KU history, and Maurice King discovered that the white players were leaving the Union and going to the Eldridge Hotel to take a nap; hotel policy prohibited black guests.

Once Chamberlain arrived, the hotel's policy suddenly changed. Aware that Chamberlain had been miffed at the kind of treatment he received when dining out with Mitt Allen, Lawrence establishments were warned that they were not to discriminate against the 7-foot star. Some things were more important than segregation—in Lawrence, basketball was one of those things.

Chapter 5
The Journey Begins

One of North Carolina's toughest games of the 1956–57 season has been largely forgotten.

Before Frank McGuire tested his team against college competition for the first time on December 4 against Furman, he scheduled an exhibition game against the AAU McCrary Eagles. The term *Amateur Athletic Union* was, in reality, a misnomer. It implied a group of amateur schoolboys, underdeveloped and undertalented.

In the mid-1950s, AAU teams offered many of the advantages that NBA teams do today. For players with little regard for a college education, they were a way to continue playing basketball without having to go to school. Players were "hired" to work at the team's jobsite—numerous big companies had a team, including Phillips 66, which had hired away Carolina's Tom Scott as head coach—but their real job was playing basketball and earning accolades for the company. What little work they did was likely to be physically demanding, so AAU teams often had more physically advanced players than the college teams they scrimmaged. The Acme-McCrary Corporation, a textile mill, sponsored the McCrary Eagles.

Carolina's game against McCrary was played in Asheboro, approximately two hours by bus in 1956, in front of a standing-room-only crowd of 1,500. The McCrary Gymnasium had not been built to accommodate large crowds. It had a stage at one end and was originally intended to be used as a recreation facility for McCrary employees. Playing in front of a gym packed with their supporters, the Eagles turned the game into a struggle. They led throughout the game before their bigger players began to accumulate foul trouble. Lennie Rosenbluth scored 6 straight points to open a 66–62 Tar Heel lead, and Carolina eventually held on for an 84–70 victory.

It was not a particularly auspicious debut for a team expected to be among the nation's best. This was supposed to be the year that the Tar Heels dethroned Everett Case and his Wolfpack. They showed why in their regular-season opener against Furman. It was one of just two games in the month of December played at Woollen Gym, and a crowd of 5,500 fans greeted the Tar Heels. (The listed capacity of Woollen would swell throughout the season as the school tried to figure out creative ways to shoehorn in as many people as possible.) With only eight opportunities to see the team in Chapel Hill, tickets were scarce.

The Tar Heels took the floor with a style befitting a Frank McGuire basketball team. One of McGuire's favorite sayings was, "It costs twenty-five cents more on the dollar to go first-class," and his team reflected that belief. Their warm-up jerseys were satin. Their warm-up pants featured buttons all the way down the side. ("When I want a boy to go into a game," McGuire said, "I want to pat him on the leg and be able to jerk those warm-ups off and yell, 'Get in the game!'") The team entered the gym to the strains of "Sweet Georgia Brown" played by a four-man, student-organized Dixieland band, a touch the head coach never would have allowed in the past. But he had been persuaded to loosen the reins somewhat, and he also believed the tune provided a bit of fun for the fans. His team used a Carolina blue-and-white basketball as they opened their layup line, a dash of color in a warm-up process that was dreary for most teams. Seeking something out of the ordinary, McGuire had also added a touch of red piping to the Tar Heel uniforms.

He held his home crowd to the same expectations of classiness. Waving one's hands during opposing free throws was explicitly discouraged, and if McGuire felt that the spectators were becoming uncouth, he would grab the public address microphone and inform them that they should be respectful at all times. In the postseason media guide released before the 1957 NCAA Tournament, the sports publicity director used the third page of the guide—after the staff listing and a brief explanation of the guide's purpose—for the following plea:

> This is a request for you to consider us as foremost candidates for the Conference's Sportsmanship Award.
>
> I believe we deserve it; and I will tell you why.
>
> In football, we probably were no better than the others. I heard of no incidents and we took all our many loses [*sic*] in good grace. In basketball, our team and student body have been really remarkable.
>
> You, no doubt, have always noticed that our basketball players have always made it a point to give the glad hand to opponents who have fouled out.
>
> Coach McGuire, in Woollen Gymnasium, repeatedly has stood up and requested the students

to be quiet when a few of our ardent supporters have gotton [*sic*] out of line with opponents on the free throw line

... Our student body had to take some hard knocks because all of the students could not see all of our big home games. Yet, they took it in stride using their priorities, and there were no demonstrations, as far as I know, that reflected on them.

The season-opening crowd was appropriately excited to see its highly touted team but also mindful of McGuire's requirements. Woollen was known for being exceptionally loud, but also for a certain element of decorum.

McGuire used a starting lineup of Rosenbluth, Pete Brennan, and Billy Hathaway in the frontcourt and Tommy Kearns and Bob Cunningham in the backcourt. Hathaway's imposing size was appealing, but even in the first game, McGuire began to use Joe Quigg off the bench for as many minutes as he played Hathaway. Fans grumbled about the use of Hathaway, believing Quigg to be the better player. McGuire met with Quigg to ascertain whether he had any problems with his role coming off the bench. The former prep star's response was simple: "Let them gripe, Coach. We know what we're doing."

The Tar Heel starting five did not appear to have much chemistry. They built just a 7-point lead at halftime over the little-known Paladins, and the Woollen crowd was murmuring. Sure, Rosenbluth had tossed in 17 first-half points, but they had seen his scoring prowess before. This was supposed to be more than just Lennie and four backups. This was supposed to be one of the best teams in the country.

McGuire juggled the lineup to start the second half, sending out Quigg in place of Hathaway. The big junior scored 10 points in the first 3:46 of the half, stretching Carolina's lead and causing a Furman defensive shift. Suddenly, the Paladins had to pay more attention to the post. That opened some gaps for Rosenbluth on the perimeter, and points started to come in bunches. First a jumper, then a hook shot, then a pullup jumper.

George "The Blind Bomber" Glamack had set the Carolina single-game scoring record with 45 points in 1941; Rosenbluth had tied that mark on two different occasions during his junior season. Now he was on the verge of breaking it. Behind Quigg and Rosenbluth, the Tar Heels stretched their lead to more than 20 points, but still McGuire left his senior superstar in the game. Sitting directly beside McGuire on the bench, team manager Joel Fleishman let the head coach know that Rosenbluth was closing in on the record. McGuire thought it would be an appropriate way to begin the season. He waited until Rosenbluth notched another basket with 54 seconds left, giving him the record-breaking 46th and 47th points, and then immediately removed him from the game. The fans, most of whom had stayed in Woollen despite the blowout, gave Rosenbluth a tremendous ovation as he left the floor.

Despite the record, news of the season-opening win was relegated to the back page of the *Daily Tar Heel*. Every football game was given prime placement on the front page directly under the masthead, but this was just a basketball game. The sold-out crowd was impressive, but the basketball team had to do more than beat Furman to capture the imagination of the campus.

Halfway across the country, Kansas also opened the season in impressive fashion—with an 87–69 victory over Northwestern. The Associated Press's breathless report on the game began this way: "Those fabulous stories about Wilt 'The Stilt' Chamberlain are true. He proved it last night."

His proof included 52 points and 31 rebounds, enough to break the conference scoring record and the Kansas rebound record. The NCAA still lists Chamberlain's 52 points as the most ever in a varsity debut; that total also stands as the Kansas single-game scoring record.

Allen Fieldhouse became the center of Chamberlain hysteria. In 1956 it ranked as the second-largest basketball arena in the country, trailing only its counterpart at the University of Minnesota. Kansas fan attendance increased by 85,000 during Chamberlain's first varsity season.

O

Today's college basketball schedules are carefully prepared documents designed to maximize a team's ability to pile up victories. The formula is simple: a few preconference cupcakes in December, perhaps a challenging holiday tournament, and conference games beginning in January. Toss in a weeklong break for exams in December and maybe one marquee nonconference game in February, and you have the general blueprint for most Division I team schedules.

The schedule wasn't quite so structured during the 1956–57 season. Just four days after the Furman contest, the Tar Heels played their first conference game of the year. The opponent was not highly regarded—although it was technically a "home" game for Clemson, the contest was held in Charlotte, a friendly environment for any Carolina team—but this was still UNC's first step on the road to repeating as regular-season champion.

The game was never in question. Carolina hit 19 of its first 25 shots on the way to a 51–36 halftime lead. Rosenbluth scored 20 points in the first 20 minutes. The Tigers, who had won just one Atlantic Coast Conference game in the league's first three seasons of existence, were very much outclassed. This time there was no need for McGuire to leave Rosenbluth in the game late, and Carolina coasted to a 94–75 victory. Pete Brennan made 9 of his 12 field goal attempts and added 11 rebounds.

Just two days later, the first Associated Press poll of the season was released. As expected, Kansas and the mythical Chamberlain were picked first. The surprise came in the rest of the top-five spots. San Francisco was ranked second, in deference to its 59-game winning streak (even though few expected the streak to continue, given that the Dons were finally without fabulous center Bill Russell). Adolph Rupp and Kentucky were ranked third, Louisville placed fourth, and little-known Southern Methodist was fifth. The Tar Heels were ranked a surprising sixth. It was still the highest ranking of any Atlantic Coast Conference team, but not close to what many Carolina fans had expected. After all, their team had ascended to fourth following the previous season's victory over Alabama, and this year's squad was expected to be much better.

The Tar Heels breezed through an 82–55 win over George Washington on December 12 in Norfolk to protect their new ranking. It was the third straight easy victory, as Carolina cruised to a 34–13 early lead and was never threatened. It was also the third straight different location for a Carolina basketball game; the fourth location in four games would come three days later when the team traveled to Columbia to face South Carolina.

After the game Rosenbluth looked at his coach and made a simple declaration: "Coach, we're going to win them all."

McGuire just hissed. He didn't want to even consider such a ludicrous thought. In the preseason a sportswriter had asked the coach about the possibility of winning every game. McGuire's response was sharp and simple: "Anyone who won them all would probably have to be cheating."

With 21 games still left on the regular-season schedule, going undefeated seemed like a dream to everyone except Rosenbluth. But the sharpshooter seemed convinced. When McGuire went over the South Carolina scouting report, he warned his team that the Gamecocks were much improved. They had previously been lumped with Clemson in a tandem of teams from south of Tobacco Road with little basketball pedigree, but they were on their way to building their first-ever over-.500 overall record since joining the ACC.

In the back of the room, Rosenbluth waved his hand. "Coach," he said, "don't worry about it. We're going to beat them."

It was to be the most formidable test of the season so far, but few in Chapel Hill had any idea of what had transpired through the first three games. There was no radio coverage of the opening trio. NC State, meanwhile, was in the process of a stunningly poor start—including losses to South Carolina and Clemson—but had enjoyed radio coverage of all its games, home and away. That the Wolfpack could find trouble both off the court with the Jackie Moreland case and on it with two unexpected losses, yet still remain the darling of the area media, was a great source of irritation for Carolina supporters.

The Tar Heel trip to South Carolina just 10 days before Christmas also received no radio coverage. The tiny Columbia gymnasium resembled a bullfighting arena more than a basketball facility; cement walls surrounded the court, and the bleachers began behind the walls. It was an unusual setup in a day when most bleachers extended all the way down to the court.

The game would mark the first of nine overtimes that Carolina would play during the season and its first dramatic come-from-behind victory. With the Tar Heels holding a 76–74 lead late in the game, South Carolina's Ray Pericola made a twisting layup with seven seconds remaining to force overtime. Pericola was an unlikely hero—he was just a sophomore and was playing in one of his first

ACC games. The real Gamecock star was Grady Wallace, who had a special knack for terrorizing the Tar Heels. Wallace had been held to just 11 points at halftime, but he exploded in the second half and finished with 35.

The overtime session spawned one of McGuire's favorite stories from 1956. No one was exactly sure whether it was completely true, but it made for terrific dinnertime comedy.

North Carolina and South Carolina have a sports rivalry born of proximity. Both believe themselves to be the "true" Carolina, and both often refer to their sports teams solely as "Carolina." It can be confusing for natives of one state who travel to the other state—particularly transplanted Tar Heels, who frequently are unaware that another school claims to be Carolina. As the Chapel Hill basketball program has grown in prominence, UNC has become the nationally accepted "Carolina," but in 1956 the issue was still in doubt.

With one minute to play in overtime and the Gamecocks holding a 2-point lead, seldom-used Tar Heel reserve Stan Groll, who would play in only 12 games all season, grabbed a rebound. McGuire whistled for a timeout. He gathered his team around him in the bandbox gym and told them to run his favorite—and, in reality, the team's only—play: give it to Rosenbluth.

The timeout ended, and both teams returned to the floor. The ball was inbounded to the 6-foot Groll, a Brooklyn native. South Carolina dropped back in a zone as the seconds dwindled. Still Groll seemed content to bounce the ball 35 feet from the basket. McGuire grew increasingly agitated as he watched his team, down by 2, act entirely too casual. He called for another timeout.

"Groll, what the hell are you doing?" he asked. "I told you to get the ball to Rosenbluth."

The sophomore playing in just his fourth varsity game looked perplexed.

"Coach, we're up by 2," he said. "I'm trying to run some time off."

It was McGuire's turn to look mystified. Then Groll pointed to the scoreboard, and the coach saw the source of the confusion.

The board read CAROLINA 86, GUEST 84.

McGuire would later tell the story with a laugh. He could afford the good humor, because his team came back to win. After the second timeout Kearns drove the lane, scored, and was fouled. He sank the free throw to provide an 87–86 advantage. After a Gamecock turnover Tony Radovich converted another three-point play to provide the eventual margin of victory.

It was the first tangible evidence of the wisdom of McGuire's "practicing with the clock" strategy. With no three-point shot and no shot clock, teams holding the lead in the closing minutes almost always managed to hold the advantage. But Carolina had remained poised facing a deficit, and even though the reliable "Get it to Rosenbluth" play had failed, another Tar Heel had stepped up to make the big shot.

The team faced a backloaded month of December that included three games in three days in New York and Boston just before Christmas, plus the post-holiday Dixie Classic. But before the Tar Heels could begin what promised to be a very telling stretch, they returned home briefly to host Maryland on December 17. It was the last home game for almost a month, as Carolina wouldn't play in Woollen again until January 11.

With Christmas break looming, the crowd was more subdued than the sellout throng that had witnessed the season opener. But the outcome was the same, as Carolina bolted to a 40–26 lead and held on for a 70–61 victory.

With his team 5–0 overall and 2–0 in the ACC, McGuire was quizzed about his squad's upcoming trip, which included a game against New York University in Madison Square Garden and back-to-back games against Dartmouth and Holy Cross in the Boston Garden.

None of the opposing teams was ranked, but McGuire remained cautious.

"If we win two out of three games up north, I'll know we have a very good team," the head coach said. "But we could very well lose them all."

O

Downplaying his team's fortunes wasn't the only way McGuire stayed in the newspapers near Christmas of 1956. Despite the disappointing, just-concluded 2–7–1 football season, there were high expectations for new gridiron coach Jim Tatum. He had the biggest office in Woollen Gym (for a short time, McGuire and Tatum actually shared an office suite, with Tatum keeping the bigger of the two offices) and was given all the support he needed by the athletic department.

McGuire wasn't accustomed to basketball being treated as a second-rate sport. He chafed at his meager accommodations in Woollen Gym, where he had an office that could not accommodate two guests at the same time. His assistant coach, Buck Freeman, used a ticket office shelf as a desk. McGuire noted that Tatum held a regular press conference at The Pines restaurant every Tuesday of the football season. Assuming that if it was good for football, it would also be beneficial for basketball, he asked that a similar press conference be held after every home basketball game. With only eight home games, McGuire felt it was a reasonable proposal.

Athletic director Chuck Erickson thought differently. He reviewed the projected expenses, considered the rationale for the press conferences, and flatly denied McGuire's request.

Erickson may have underestimated the power his head basketball coach held with the local media. Sportswriters loved him—in addition to being a great quote, he knew how to take care of them. Being denied an opportunity to dine with him at The Pines meant losing not only a chance to create more editorial copy, but also a meal at one of the best restaurants in Chapel Hill.

McGuire never spoke about the press conference snub publicly. But he did "accidentally" mention it to Hugo Germino, the sports editor of the *Durham Sun*. Within a few days Germino had penned a story exposing the "strife stricken UNC athletic department." Germino chose his words carefully, and the implication was clear: Tatum was somehow behind Erickson's decision regarding basketball. The football coach wanted to keep football at the top of the department's hierarchy and keep basketball in its rightful place in the Woollen Gym basement. Included in Germino's story was a shuddering thought for the loyal base of Carolina basketball fans: McGuire wasn't happy with the treatment he was receiving and might be tempted to leave for an offer in the big city if the situation was not rectified. Of course, Germino didn't have that sentiment in a quote from McGuire. But everyone knew that he had heard it directly from the coach.

The perceived slights were accumulating rapidly on McGuire's desk. He had scheduled the northern road swing as a chance to increase his program's exposure in his primary recruiting territories and give many of his players a chance to perform in the arena they considered the mecca of college basketball, Madison Square Garden. It also helped that McGuire himself would have plenty of friends in New York City for the game against NYU. Noting that Tatum had taken close friends from the Carolina administration on football road trips, he requested the addition of two close university friends to the basketball team's traveling party to New York.

The request was denied.

Once the *Durham Sun* exposed the story, the *Daily Tar Heel* immediately jumped into the fray.

Columnist Neil Bass sounded the first warning siren. "Is there a big shake-up in store for the Athletic Department?" his December 14 column began. "Does Carolina stand a strong chance of losing amiable basketball mentor Frank McGuire? Is the Athletic Department administration undergoing complete revision to suit the Tatumian taste?"

The column went on to detail several affronts to basketball at Carolina. The status of Woollen Gym again became an issue, including Erickson's rumored promise upon hiring McGuire that a new Tar Heel basketball facility would be operational within five years. Not only was no such facility forthcoming, there had been no talk of an upgrade.

Erickson, the student paper believed, emphasized football at the expense of all other sports. It also was suggested that Tatum was behind many of the decisions to deny basketball expenses. With an important three-game road trip over Christmas break approaching, the school made no effort to secure tickets for students. An enterprising student had to begin the push, using his own funds to purchase a block of seats. There were even rumors that McGuire's players had been asked not to eat at the Monogram Club, the dining establishment for athletes on campus. Instead, the story went, they had been banished to Lenoir Hall.

All these transgressions were pinned on Tatum, but the football coach was curiously silent. It was later revealed that he had been in Wilmington recruiting and, in an era of much less media saturation, was isolated from the firestorm brewing back home. When he returned to Chapel Hill, Tatum was summoned to a three-hour meeting that included himself, sports publicity director Jake Wade, Erickson, and McGuire. All parties emerged from the meeting with bright smiles, and the headline in the next *Daily Tar Heel* (above the masthead this time) read MCGUIRE AND TATUM DENY SPLIT REPORTS. Despite Bass's reference to Tatum in print as a "parasitic monster," everything was once again copasetic in the land of Tar Heel athletics.

But an interesting precedent had been established. Tatum had come to Carolina a conquering hero. He was a UNC alum, had spent several successful years at Maryland, and had won a national championship there. His hiring was supposed to signal a return to football prominence for North Carolina.

Just a few months after his arrival, however, he was engaged in a war with the school's head basketball coach—and losing the battle of perception. Students were not naturally predisposed to favor basketball; after all, many arrived at the school with little background in the sport. But McGuire's congenial attitude—coupled with a bushel of wins and a healthy outlook for the future of the program—had won them over. In a war between basketball and football, there was for the first time an indication that the campus might be willing to back hoops.

○

In addition to being one of the few early-season occasions when Carolina games would be broadcast on the radio—a six-station network that included WBBB in Burlington, WDNC in Durham, and WBIG in Greensboro picked up all three games—the trip north represented an important milestone for Carolina's reserves. Since the beginning of the year, McGuire had encouraged Stan Groll, Tony Radovich, and Danny Lotz with the same refrain: "By the Dartmouth game, you guys will be starting!"

That was all the incentive the fun-loving Radovich needed. Every day in practice, he would creep up to Lotz and shout, "Hey, Danny, is it the Dartmouth game yet?" The reserves probably knew that they had little chance of displacing the Tar Heel starters, but the charade continued. In McGuire's world, of course, being a starter meant considerable minutes—four or five times the minutes of anyone on the bench. From his seat there Radovich would watch the Tar Heels blow away the early-season opponents and ask, just loud enough for McGuire to hear, "Is it the Dartmouth game yet?" The coach would fume, the reserves would laugh, and the starters would continue bludgeoning the opponent.

Finally, after a 64–59 Carolina win over NYU in Madison Square Garden, it was the Dartmouth game. The Big Green, an Ivy League school, was little competition for Carolina on the hardwood. Groll, Radovich, and Lotz didn't crack the starting lineup, but they had high hopes for significant minutes in what promised to be a blowout. The Tar Heels stretched their lead beyond 20 points in the first half, and Rosenbluth passed Al Lifson for Carolina's all-time scoring lead while pouring in 30 points. Lotz and Radovich elbowed each other on the bench. This was their chance.

"Tony must've said it 50 times in that game," Lotz recalls. "'Hey, Danny, is this the Dartmouth game?'"

Finally, with a minute to play and Carolina holding a 30-point lead, McGuire grudgingly inserted the reserves. Radovich, naturally, knew exactly what to say: "This must be the Dartmouth game!"

When they got on the floor, Radovich, Lotz, and Groll could barely suppress their laughter. The game was long since decided, and the Boston Garden crowd probably wondered what was so funny. But McGuire knew. After the 89–61 victory, he unloaded on the trio in the locker room. With snow swirling outside, he informed them that they would not be welcome on the team bus. Still laughing about their plight, the young men hitchhiked back to the team hotel.

It was December 21, 1956. Montgomery, Alabama, had just ended race-based seat assignments on city buses. After an easy victory the next day over Holy Cross, Carolina would enter the Christmas break at 8–0. One of the biggest events of the season, the Dixie Classic, loomed.

Southwest of Chapel Hill, a young fan cut out newspaper photos of his new favorite team for the first time and put them on his wall. They were head shots of McGuire and Rosenbluth, the poster boys for Carolina basketball. Woody Durham, who was still 15 years away from beginning a nearly four-decade career as the radio voice of the Tar Heels, still cannot explain what made him save the photos.

"I had never done anything like that before," he says. "But this was a team that was really creating some excitement. We were all starting to get caught up in what this team might be able to do."

Chapter 6

A Christmas Ritual

Across America in December 1956, most boys had a simple Christmas list. Some wanted Lincoln Logs or a Schwinn bicycle. The more adventurous might have asked for a cowboy outfit to emulate their heroes on *Gunsmoke*, which aired on CBS and was one of the most popular television shows of the year. American Flyer and Lionel electric train sets were trendy gifts. Stereo vinyl records wouldn't be released for two more years, but that didn't prevent Dean Martin from recording the nation's top song of the year—"Memories Are Made of This." Elvis Presley checked in at number five with "Heartbreak Hotel."

Somewhere in America, boys might have been content to find a Martin or Presley record under the tree. Not in Chapel Hill, North Carolina. Not in Raleigh. And not in Durham. On Tobacco Road there was only one present on every Christmas list: tickets to the Dixie Classic.

The three-day, eight-team tournament held—where else?—at Reynolds Coliseum immediately after Christmas had all the perfect elements of drama. The permanent hosts were the four Tobacco Road teams: NC State, Carolina, Wake Forest, and Duke. Those squads played host to a rotating list of the nation's top basketball power-houses. The idea, which had been hatched by Case, was pure genius. For 362 days out of the year, the teams on Tobacco Road ganged up on each other. State fans cheered against Carolina fans, who in turn cheered against Wake, who in turn cheered against Duke. Case wanted to figure out a way to harness that negative energy and turn it into something more positive.

The Dixie Classic was born. For three days out of the year, fans of the Big Four schools banded together against the interlopers. Local partisans wanted their own team to win, of course, but if their squad was eliminated, they switched loyalties to another state team. Even the name, Dixie, was native. No one wanted some bunch of outsiders—or worse, a bunch of Yankees! (any Yankees wearing Carolina blue were considered to be adopted and therefore acceptable to the masses)—to come in and win the North Carolina–based tournament. Southerners were still very much looked down upon; this was their opportunity to deal out some punishment on the hardwood. The postseason con-ference tournament was a chance to compete against each other; the Dixie Classic was a chance to compete against the nation.

Everett Case looked like a genius when his Wolfpack won the first four tournaments. The prestige of the event grew rapidly, and even though outsiders knew that they were unlikely to win the whole tour-nament—no team from outside the Big Four ever won the event in its 12-year history—they kept making the trip to Raleigh. Case oversaw every detail, ensuring that teams were treated with Southern hospitality and that the area's best officials were used to keep control of some potentially combustible games. In an era when intersectional non-conference games were a rarity, some of the nation's finest players—including Cincinnati's Oscar Robertson and Michigan State's Johnny Green—passed through Reynolds Coliseum for the Dixie Classic.

There were other holiday tournaments. Kentucky held the Kentucky Invitational, the event that perhaps most closely resembled the Dixie Classic in terms of prestige. But the Bluegrass State lacked the tight core of competitive teams available in North Carolina. Kansas played in the Big Seven Holiday Tournament, conveniently held in Kansas City's Municipal Auditorium, the future site of the 1957 national championship game. The Jayhawks won a close battle in the 1956 tournament opener, claiming a 58–57 decision over Iowa State, and then easily defeated Oklahoma and Colorado to win the title. But despite the proximity to Lawrence, the tournament was not sold out.

The Dixie Classic had no problem getting rid of tickets. In an effort to make the bracket as fair as possible, Big Four teams drew names the week before the event. That led to some colossal mismatches (Carolina lost three straight games in the tournament in Frank McGuire's second year, when the draw was unfavorable) but also created a feeling of excitement about the pairings.

"I've met a lot of people who tell me that when they were growing up, their only Christmas present was an opportunity to go to the Dixie Classic with their father," Bob Cunningham says. "That was the best Christmas present they could ever receive. The place was a madhouse."

It was a madhouse with a distinctly red tint. NC State had started a unique group known as the Wolfpack Club. The idea was simple but innovative: A group of men who enjoyed NC State athletics supported Wolfpack teams financially and with their attendance at sporting events. One of the perks of membership was a bright red blazer.

Wolfpack Club members would perch in the few sideline seats at Reynolds (because of a construction quirk, the arena had many more seats behind the baskets than on the sides of the court) clad in their blazers, creating a bright red boundary around anyone standing on the court. Today, the words *booster club* conjure images of a moneyed crowd spending as much time discussing corporate affairs as the game. In the infancy of the groups, however, they were essentially rabid clubs for fans willing to pay for the privilege. Business might have been conducted during the Dixie Classic, but not while the ball was in play.

Technically, the post-Christmas games were not road games for North Carolina teams playing in the NC State arena. Even today, UNC's media guide lists games played there as "Raleigh" rather than the "Away" designation given to true road games. But players knew different—any Wolfpack loss was considered an upset. Carolina had entered the 1955 tournament ranked fourth in the country. The team whipped Alabama and then thumped eighth-ranked Duke in the semifinals to force a championship showdown against third-ranked State. Behind talented junior Lennie Rosenbluth and with a frisky class of sophomores, the Tar Heels had decided that it was their year to finally break through and win the Dixie Classic.

"You walked in there, and you saw nothing but red," Cunningham remembers. "State ran it, they controlled it, and on top of all that, they were a very good program—so everything was in their favor. We went in there, and we were feeling pretty cocky about ourselves. But State had a great team, and they had us down by 16 points at halftime. They really did a number on us. The embarrassment of losing so badly in front of all those State fans really upset all of us."

In that Reynolds locker room, listening to the Wolfpack fans and players celebrate, the returning Tar Heels had made a pact: This would not be allowed to happen again.

O

Carolina drew Utah in the 1956 quarterfinals. Across the country San Francisco had suffered a loss that snapped a 62-game winning streak; as a result, the Tar Heels had moved up to second in the most recent Associated Press poll. There was some concern about a letdown in front of a partially hostile crowd, but the worries were unfounded. Carolina easily defeated Utah 97–76. And it turned out to be perhaps the most friendly crowd the Tar Heels had ever encountered in Reynolds Coliseum. As usual, local fans cheered passionately for their teams and then rooted for the other North Carolina squads in their quarterfinal games. It was a basketball-centric example of the big brother/little brother syndrome: We might pick on those other guys the rest of the year, but we don't let anyone else do it.

Few fans bought tickets for individual games. Instead, they bought the full tournament package: passes for all 12 games sandwiched into the same ticket book. Because it was a no-elimination tournament—every team was guaranteed three games, which helped persuade national programs to attend—fans had no reason to pack up and leave when their team lost. A defeat meant only a different matchup the next day. (One of the greatest contests in Dixie Classic history was actually a consolation game, as fourth-ranked Carolina defeated second-ranked Cincinnati, featuring Oscar Robertson, 90–88 for third place in 1959.)

The 1956–57 Tar Heels had no interest in a potential consolation game. After throttling Utah they faced ninth-ranked Duke. It was exactly what area fans hoped for—all four local teams won their quarterfinal games, creating the dream Dixie semifinals: Carolina vs. Duke in one semifinal, State vs. Wake in the other. They weren't officially conference games, as they would not count in the league standings, but it was an early chance to see the only four teams that had finished above .500 in the league the season before. With any luck, fans thought, it would be a preview of the ACC Tournament semifinals.

In any other year a Carolina–NC State final would have been the marquee attraction. But the Wolfpack was struggling by their own standards, and with Wake Forest returning a senior-laden team, the Deacs looked like a capable challenger to Carolina. Memories of the ACC Tournament embarrassment the season before, when Wake beat Carolina 77–56, were still fresh.

For the second straight year, Carolina eased past Duke in the semifinals, claiming its third win over a top-10 team in the past two seasons. Wake toppled State, compounding Case's misery, as he had to watch two of his biggest rivals square off in the championship game of his showcase event.

This time, the Tar Heels and Demon Deacons made it through an entire game without fighting. In their four meetings during the course of the season, it was the only time that Wake wasn't ranked in the top 20.

Carolina emerged with a 63–55 victory and claimed its first Dixie Classic championship. Fans celebrated with a fervor usually reserved for ACC titles. It would be hard to imagine a better script for Carolina: NC State loses in the semifinals, Carolina wins the title, and Case has to watch McGuire and his team snip the nets in Reynolds Coliseum.

McGuire's Tar Heels would go on to win the event two more times (in 1958 and 1961) before a point-shaving scandal ended the tradition. With Case's program already reeling from the Jackie Moreland probation, allegations of gamblers infiltrating the popular Classic incensed university system president William Friday. Four Wolfpack players were indicted for point-shaving, and the venerable Friday ordered a de-emphasis of basketball at the system's two most prominent schools: State and Carolina.

All the Tar Heels involved in the 1956 Dixie Classic said gamblers played no role in that tournament. With State usually racking up victories, it was too important an event to risk losing on purpose.

As the calendar flipped to 1957—it was still 15 years before a man named Dick Clark would consider hosting a New Year's Eve television show; even *American Bandstand* had not started yet—the Tar Heels were 11–0 and ranked second in the country. They had claimed victories at seven different venues and already had three conference wins.

The Chapel Hill campus was shuttered for winter break as the Dixie Classic concluded. When it reopened in early January 1957, few had any idea that it was about to be transformed into the center of the college basketball universe.

Chapter 7

Inside the Smoking Car

Frank McGuire looked at his team's early January schedule and saw trouble.

For McGuire this wasn't unusual. He was a typical coach and could locate trouble almost anywhere. This time, it wasn't a particular opponent that concerned him. Instead, it was the lack of an opponent. After capturing the Dixie Classic title, the Tar Heels had more than a week off before traveling to Williamsburg to face William & Mary.

Worried about the potential ill effects of the break, he put his team through a full scrimmage, varsity squad against the freshman squad, on January 6. Just like in the preseason, it was a less-than-impressive performance by the varsity, as they mustered only an 80–69 victory.

The struggles continued in Williamsburg on January 8 in front of a standing-room-only crowd of 3,000. (By then the Tar Heels were drawing capacity crowds wherever they went.) William & Mary controlled the tempo and built a 28–26 halftime lead. For the second time in a month—he had also struggled against NYU, mustering just 9 points against the Violets' physical brand of defense—Lennie Rosenbluth was in the throes of an off night. McGuire needed someone, anyone, to shoulder some of the offensive load. He turned to scrappy Tommy Kearns. Carolina surged at the start of the second half and took a 5-point lead, but the Indians drew within 51–47 with eight minutes to play. With William & Mary focusing on Rosenbluth, Kearns was able to penetrate into the lane; he converted four straight layups to help the Tar Heels hold on for a 71–61 victory.

For the high-scoring Rosenbluth, any sub-30-point game was cause for concern. Wake Forest assistant coach Bones McKinney wondered publicly if Carolina's star was underweight. Although the Tar Heels wouldn't admit it, McKinney was right. The already slender Rosenbluth was 15 pounds under his playing weight and seemed to be dropping more pounds every day. Like most of his teammates, he believed that working out with weights during the season would negatively impact his jump shot. Coaches usually warned their players against any extra conditioning; they wanted basketball players, not weightlifters.

Rosenbluth found this an easy edict to follow. He was the classic example of a player who looked listless in practice but found another gear when the game began.

"He didn't like to practice," Bob Cunningham says. "He was honest about that."

Rosenbluth explained his aversion to casual, nongame play by espousing one of his pet theories: If a player was going to get hurt, it would be when he faced players who were not as good as he was. Growing up in New York, Rosenbluth had seen too many playground hacks come down on someone's ankle or undercut a more athletic player while he was leaping to the hoop.

Rosenbluth's teammates were somewhat skeptical of this rationale. One evening, the squad assembled for practice on the court of Woollen Gym, only to find Rosenbluth lying flat on his back on the wooden bleachers. Word spread quickly through the team: He was trying to shake yet another one of his colds, which always seemed to flare up during practices rather than games. McGuire secured two towels from manager Joel Fleishman, then walked over to his prone superstar and placed the towels over Rosenbluth's face. The team dissolved into laughter. Rosenbluth never moved. He would remain on the wooden bench for the remainder of practice, in the same position.

Rosenbluth's concern for his health extended to the team's eating arrangements. Although McGuire's taste for finer restaurants was well known, the meager basketball budget did not allow for cloth napkins and fine china. Instead, the Tar Heels usually had to make the best of whatever roadside diner was available. On one occasion the bus pulled up to an establishment that was, by the standards of the day, better than average. The head coach had done some scouting and made reservations in advance.

McGuire and most of his players were encouraged. "This looks like a fine place," the coach said.

Rosenbluth was not so sure. He peered out the window and evaluated the conditions. Once again, he was playing the role of the crusty old codger who was older and wiser than his youthful teammates.

"It looks to me like a great place to pick up a case of ptomaine," he replied with a skeptical eye.

It was unusual for the team to be on the bus in the first place. Typically, bus trips were only for closer road games such as NC State, Wake Forest, and Duke. For anything outside state lines, the team bundled into two mammoth DeSoto station wagons. McGuire and the rest of the staff were always in the same car together, often with some of the players. But assignment to a specific station wagon was not by class, playing time, or anything else related to basketball. Instead, it was a much simpler dividing line: smokers in one car, nonsmokers in the other.

Joe Quigg, he of Marlboro representation, was in the smoking car. Others who occasionally joined that group were Rosenbluth, Cunningham, Tommy Kearns, and Pete Brennan. They were often quick to note in the presence of their head coach that they themselves, naturally, didn't plan to smoke. They just wanted to be in the same car with their buddies. McGuire had good reason to be suspicious of that claim—after all, anyone passing by the wagons on the road would note that while one had the windows rolled up, the other had the windows rolled down, with fumes escaping from inside.

Flights to road games were extremely limited and usually approved only for games outside the immediate Atlantic Coast Conference area. The circumstances gnawed at McGuire, who would have preferred only the best arrangements. He had not grown up with money but easily made observers assume otherwise. One of the gifts that made him so effective in a recruit's home was his ability to be all things to all people. In a hardscrabble neighborhood, he could tell stories about a rough childhood and plenty of hungry nights. In a more formal setting, he could provide hours of dinner conversation and make an eloquent toast. He knew that the football team traveled more lavishly than the basketball squad—even though the former had many more players to accommodate—but he wanted to notch more wins before he raised the issue in public.

O

While Carolina traveled across the region to accumulate more wins, Kansas was also piling up victories. The Jayhawks won their first dozen games, most by double figures. Their star player was a devastating force on both offense and defense. On defense Jayhawks coach Dick Harp stationed Chamberlain near the basket, where he could block shots—or, at minimum, alter the shots of Kansas opponents—and grab every rebound.

While on offense KU faced numerous different strategies as opponents tried to unlock the mystery to holding Chamberlain under 30 points. Teams had not yet decided how to defend a 7-footer who could not only shoot and rebound over their biggest player, but also outrun some of the opposing guards. Many teams in the East played zone, but the Midwest was still man-to-man territory. Matching one man against Chamberlain quickly proved to be pointless.

"Teams were very cautious against Wilt," Kansas assistant coach Jerry Waugh says. "He was such a presence in and around the basket. As the season progressed, the defenses we saw became more and more innovative. One popular one was for teams to play a one-three-one [zone], with one man behind Wilt and one in front of him. They wanted to limit his movement, and they body checked him a lot."

That physical play would eventually be one of the factors that drove Chamberlain out of the college game one year early. In a relatively free-flowing era, he had to endure plenty of contact. The college game had just two officials, so their court coverage was limited. It was simple human nature to view the enormous Chamberlain as capable of taking more punishment than the average player.

"He'd run down the court, and people would jump out in front of him if he wasn't looking to try and draw a foul," Waugh recalls. "All the official would see would be Wilt running over a guy, and of course if you see this 7-footer running over a 6-footer, then the foul is on the 7-footer."

Most of the Big Seven Conference provided little competition for Kansas. But Iowa State had already proven to be a tricky opponent, having played the Jayhawks in a close game during the holiday tournament. The Cyclones became one of the first teams to effectively execute what would become a very popular game plan against Chamberlain: slow the tempo, take advantage of the lack of rules governing the length of a possession, and play efficient offense long enough to edge out to a meager lead.

"Once people realized what Wilt could do, the game very quickly went into a walking game," Waugh says. "Our opponents decided they were simply not going to play up-tempo basketball against Kansas. We had good support players, but Wilt himself was so devastating when he was allowed to go up and down the floor. He was like a giraffe. He looked so effortless that sometimes it appeared he wasn't running very hard, but he could cover a lot of ground in a hurry."

Iowa State was well aware of Chamberlain's athletic ability. So on January 14, with a raucous crowd behind them, the Cyclones tried to control the clock against Kansas. Slowing the tempo was an effective way to hold down the big man's raw numbers, but it also required the slowing team to take advantage of every available offensive possession. No layups could be missed, no free throws botched. For one night in Ames, Iowa State did everything right and eked out a 39–37 victory.

The shock waves were felt all the way to Chapel Hill. It seemed fairly elementary: Kansas had been ranked number one, Carolina number two. The Jayhawks had lost, so if the Tar Heels remained undefeated, they would ascend to the top spot in the Associated Press poll for the first time ever.

The next morning, word spread quickly: Kansas had lost! UNC had already breezed past Clemson and Virginia on back-to-back nights in Woollen Gym, with the Tigers falling 86–54 and the Cavaliers losing a racehorse 102–90 game. Neither of those programs could reasonably expect to compete against the rising power in Chapel Hill.

To make the jump from rising power to true power, however, the Tar Heels would have to get past their next opponent: Everett Case and NC State at Reynolds Coliseum. The Pack was experiencing a surprisingly poor season and had just an 8–6 record. But only one of those losses, a defeat at the hands of Wake Forest, had come in Reynolds. McGuire had almost exorcised some of his Case-created demons in the spring of 1956: The Tar Heels built a 10-point lead in Reynolds but subsequently tightened up and suffered a 79–73 defeat. This time, there was even more at stake—an edge in the rivalry, an important ACC victory, and national prestige.

January 15, 1957, marked the first time in 10 years (a period in which the Pack held the overall series record lead, 24–3) that Carolina was favored over a homestanding NC State squad. It was also one of the few times that the Tar Heels would not be forced to slow the tempo and hold the ball in an effort to keep the game close. This time, they had the personnel advantage, and it grew even more significant in the days before the game. Case was forced to play without sophomore John Richter, one of State's most valuable rebounders and scorers, who had sprained his ankle. The stars seemed to be aligning for an important Carolina victory.

The game came in the middle of an atypical North Carolina winter weather surge. Ice began to pelt the area, but still a sellout crowd made it to Reynolds in time for the 8:15 p.m. tip-off. What the fans saw must have looked like a mirage: It was State rather than Carolina that had to hold the ball to control the score. The Wolfpack were successful in milking the clock but unsuccessful in building a lead. The Tar Heels put the first 8 points on the board; State didn't make a field goal until 10:34 remained in the first half. The teams traded baskets over the final 10 minutes of the half, and Carolina went to the locker room with a 28–23 advantage.

"I'll be honest, all the players were pretty pleased," Pete Brennan remembers. "Here we are playing for the number one ranking in the country, and we are up on State on their court by 5 points.

"Then McGuire comes into the locker room. He goes crazy, absolutely crazy. If you could punch your coach, that's what we wanted to do. He left us all feeling that way. But he just wanted to make sure we didn't relax. He didn't want us to feel like we had won the game just because we were ahead by 5 points. At the time, I think we all disagreed with what he was doing because it left us feeling like we were losing the game."

Shortly after McGuire's explosion, his team almost did find itself behind. State closed the deficit to 53–50 with just seven minutes remaining. It looked like another example of Case's wizardry against North Carolina. He had his worst team in several years, Carolina had its best, and he was somehow going to pull the upset.

But Rosenbluth and Brennan would not allow it. They combined to make 11 straight free throws to stretch the lead to 64–54. State, already playing without Richter, lost its other main inside force when Bob Seitz, a 6-foot-11 center from New Jersey, fouled out. That left the Wolfpack without any inside presence, and they suffered from the height disadvantage immediately. Carolina scored 30 points over the final seven minutes of the game and cruised to an 83–57 victory. It was the largest Tar Heel margin of victory in the series since a 71–34 win on January 23, 1946. It also marked the last game for reserve Tony Radovich, who scored 11 points in his Carolina finale. Radovich, a January enrollee whose sense of humor made him enormously popular with his teammates, had exhausted his eligibility.

Unlike his first victory in Reynolds, this time McGuire did not allow his team to cut down the nets. But a sizable contingent of Carolina fans had made the trip to Raleigh, and they cheered the team lustily as the squad boarded the bus to go back to Chapel Hill. Ice was still pelting down, making driving conditions treacherous. Very few drivers in North Carolina had chains on their tires, and the slippery roads wreaked havoc with the victory caravan as soon as it departed

Raleigh. After a slow, frustrating drive, the team was approximately halfway home when a car making the turn from Raleigh Road onto Highway 54 fishtailed, coming to rest in the middle of the road. The team bus—and close to 100 Carolina fans—were trapped behind the waylaid car and unable to move.

A handful of fans with the benefit of chains took a detour and went through Durham. Many of the rest did the only thing they could—start walking.

"I will never forget that," Cunningham says. "Everybody was sliding off the road and our bus did, too. So we all get out of the car, and everyone is walking with us. Nobody's car could get down the highway. So we just get into a group, and we're singing and laughing and carrying on as we walk. It's midnight, our bus is in a ditch somewhere, and absolutely nobody cared."

Those who were hesitant to leave their cars behind still found a way to share their Tar Heel pride in a team that had won the first 15 games of the season by an average of 17.2 points per game.

"We skidded to a stop behind a long, piled-up line of cars returning to Chapel Hill and got out to stretch our legs," McGuire told the *New York Times* the next day. "We were recognized immediately and, in a matter of minutes, we were in the center of the biggest impromptu pep rally you can imagine.

"It was still going strong, complete with a bonfire, two hours later when the sanding trucks had finally made the road passable again.

"You expect your rooting section to whoop it up during a game but that kind of support really comes from the heart and it's bound to make you play a little better."

Nevertheless, McGuire was nervous that some members of that boisterous rooting section were beginning to let their expectations get too high. During his tenure at Carolina, his teams had yet to even play in an ACC Tournament championship game, much less win one and advance to the NCAA Tournament.

"There's just one thing wrong with it," he said. "Those people are sure we won't lose a game. I'm afraid they're going to be disappointed on that count. I'll be happy if we can go the rest of the way losing only three or four."

Not counting a post-exams tune-up against Western Carolina on January 30 (a game Carolina would win easily, 77–59), McGuire's team had just eight regular-season games remaining. It sounded like classic coachspeak. But McGuire was legitimately concerned that there was too much discussion of faraway dreams such as undefeated seasons, ACC championships, and a potential matchup with Kansas. Fans were talking about it; his players were talking about it. A fraternity brother of several Tar Heels remembers sitting around a dorm room with a handful of players and hearing them discuss, in surprising detail given the era, Kansas's roster.

Even the head coach was forced to think about it. When the new issue of *Sports Illustrated* became available at the downtown Franklin Street newsstand, the publication suggested that despite the loss, Kansas was still the nation's best team. A group of angry Carolina students collected all the copies they could find. There, in the middle of the bench-lined square of asphalt that served as the hub of campus activity, they held a bonfire to protest the egregious injustice that had been done to the Tar Heels.

The hype for a potential Carolina-Kansas battle was beginning to gurgle to the surface. No matter that in those days of strictly regional postseason seeding, the teams could meet only in a national semifinal or championship game. Two days after the win at State, the *Daily Tar Heel* ran a story headlined KANSAS, UNC MEETING SAID NOT LIKELY.

"We'd have to build a fence around Wilt Chamberlain," McGuire said. "We'd have to come up with some sort of zone to worry him."

The head coach made it clear, though, that he had more pressing concerns than a 7-footer in another conference.

"I think we could lose as many as three in a row because we're in a very tough conference," he said. "By no stretch of the imagination do I expect us to go undefeated. I believe it's better to lose a few games at the first anyway. That way you're more relaxed."

McGuire had little choice but to remain relaxed—his family saw to that. After the win over NC State, a newspaper heralded Carolina's ascension to the nation's top ranking. His daughter Patsy ran into the den brandishing the paper.

"Daddy, you're number one!" she said.

Just as he was about to accept her congratulations and perhaps allow himself a brief moment of satisfaction, a voice wafted into the den from the kitchen. The coach's other daughter, Carol Ann, no doubt having heard her father express the exact same sentiment on numerous occasions, quickly injected some reality into the family.

"There's only one way to go now, Daddy, isn't there?"

Chapter 8

"Carolina Is About to Get Beat!"

The path to defending the nation's top ranking began in Maryland. The Terrapins were the only non–Big Four team to infiltrate the top half of the Atlantic Coast Conference during its first three seasons of existence, and they were playing equally well in the 1957 season. Behind head coach Bud Millikan, Maryland had already notched home wins over Wake Forest, NC State, and Duke; a win over Carolina would be one of the program's biggest victories and secure an unprecedented season of success against the ACC's marquee teams.

The two teams had a history of close games—the last six contests between them had been decided by an average of 6 points. The Terrapins had pulled out a shocker at home in 1955, as they converted a disputed steal and turnover into the game-winning layup for a 63–61 victory. McGuire was irate after the game and stormed into the locker room, where he proceeded to question his team's toughness, manhood, and every other intangible imaginable.

"We do not lose like this at the buzzer!" he said. "At North Carolina we do not let this happen!"

A year later, the teams played another close game in College Park. This time, however, there was no late steal for Maryland, and Carolina held on for a 68–62 victory. McGuire again returned to the locker room with his team, but with an entirely different demeanor. He knew exactly what to say to make the Tar Heels revel in their accomplishment.

"I'm so proud of you boys," he said with a smile. "Chapel Hill is going to be very happy about the outcome of this game. The entire state is going to be so proud of you."

McGuire's opponent on the bench, Millikan, was also trying to build a program. He had overseen Maryland's move from tiny Ritchie Coliseum into the enormous Cole Field House, a facility with few equals. Originally known as the Student Activities Building when it opened in 1955, it gave Maryland the only arena in the ACC that rivaled Reynolds Coliseum. Expansion would later grow capacity to 14,596, but the venue originally held 12,000 fans, still an impressive number when the Tar Heels arrived in College Park by train on February 5, 1957. The arena was in its first season as Cole Field House, having been renamed to honor Judge William P. Cole Jr., a former university administrator.

"To that point, that was the biggest game ever played in the South," Bob Cunningham recalls. "It was like the inauguration game for Cole Field House. We walked in there, and it was like the Roman Coliseum. They smelled blood, man. They wanted it so bad they could taste it."

After struggling to find any coverage of their team as recently as just one month previous, fans now could follow the Tar Heels through a variety of traveling media. WPTF, the goliath of North Carolina radio stations with 50,000-watt power and the valuable AM signal (car radios were almost exclusively AM at the time), sent play-by-play man Jim Reid to cover the event. The game was such big news that it even overshadowed a report that Carolina football coach Jim Tatum, after a long flirtation with Indiana, had turned down the Hoosiers' head-coaching job. In the middle of winter, basketball had finally caught up with football in North Carolina.

Fans listening to the game back in the Tar Heel State probably needed a pencil with a good eraser to keep up with their team. After Joe Quigg replaced him in the starting lineup, Billy Hathaway paid less attention to his studies. Grade problems eventually made him ineligible, and he left the team the weekend before the trip to Maryland. He would later resurface at the University of Dayton. The squad had already lost Radovich at midseason due to the expiration of his eligibility. McGuire had planned to fill Radovich's reserve slot with Stan Groll, but Groll also encountered academic problems and withdrew from school. He would never play another game for the Tar Heels.

The team picture taken at the beginning of the season bore little resemblance to the squad that took the floor in College Park. (In all, Carolina would take four team pictures during the 1956–57 season due to the constant revolving door in Woollen Gym.) McGuire was down to just nine players: Cunningham, Lennie Rosenbluth, Joe Quigg, Tommy Kearns, Pete Brennan, Danny Lotz, Roy Searcy, Ken Rosemond, and Gehrmann Holland. At 6-foot-7, Lotz was the only post player among the reserves.

It wasn't quite as bad as McGuire's first season, when he had to dress out a manager just to have a full bench, but he knew that he would eventually need more depth in the paint. And he knew exactly where to find it.

Bob Young was a 6-foot-6 senior who had seen action in 36 games over his sophomore and junior seasons. He was expected to be one of the key reserves—if the starter-loving McGuire ever really had "key reserves"—during his senior campaign. But just before his senior season, he found himself in jail after an encounter with the Chapel Hill police. The first person to come see him was his head coach.

"Well," McGuire said with a solemn shake of his head, "if this doesn't motivate you to do the right thing, nothing ever will."

Young's scholarship was revoked, and he was forbidden to practice with the team. To earn money the Queens native worked in the Monogram Club and the Carolina Inn. Instead of working out at Woollen Gym with the team, he had to try to keep in shape alone at the team's former home court, the Indoor Athletic Center—better known to everyone in town as the Tin Can.

McGuire, intent on making sure one of his New York boys did not run aground in Chapel Hill, stayed in contact with Young. There was no talk of his basketball scholarship, just talk of work and staying in shape and—most often—staying out of trouble.

"It was a humbling experience," Young recalls. "I had periodic visits with him, and he really became a fatherlike figure to me."

Unbeknownst to Young, this figure was also lobbying for his reinstatement. Even then, absent the millions of dollars and expansive television coverage that have swallowed modern college basketball, Carolina administrators were hesitant to present the image that a basketball player was getting special treatment. McGuire believed that Young deserved to be reinstated; dean of students Ray Jefferies was not so certain. After numerous meetings Jefferies finally relented just before the Tar Heels were set to depart for College Park. McGuire contacted Young to relay the good news: He was back on scholarship, back on the team, and needed immediately for the trip to Maryland.

NCAA rules permitted teams to carry a maximum of 18 scholarship players. McGuire usually liked to have around 15, leaving plenty of room in case a midyear high school graduate (Joe Quigg being a prime example) wanted to join the team in January. But McGuire was staring at an enormous cushion for the final two months of the 1957 season. As he loaded his team onto the train for the trip to Maryland, he counted just 10 scholarship players.

The Terrapins packed a capacity crowd, one of the most raucous environments Carolina would face all season, into Cole for the 8:00 p.m. tip-off. The Tuesday game coincided with a traditional night for high school basketball in North Carolina, creating some conflicted fans. At Albemarle High School, 100 miles from Chapel Hill, Woody Durham was sitting behind a microphone working the public address system. It was a girls and boys doubleheader; the girls game was nearly complete when the clock started in College Park.

Top-ranked Carolina was getting its toughest challenge since assuming the number one ranking. With two minutes left in regulation and the Tar Heels trailing by 2 points, McGuire called timeout and huddled his team around him. Noise from the sellout crowd was deafening.

"Our streak had to end sometime, and this looks like it," McGuire told his squad. "So, fellows, let's lose graciously. When the horn goes off, go right over and congratulate those Maryland boys."

After hearing the head coach speak, manager Joel Fleishman, who was in charge of keeping the scorebook, flipped it shut. The coach had essentially conceded. Shouldn't the scorekeeper? It was the first and only time all season that he closed it before the end of a game.

In Albemarle a late-arriving fan walked into the gym. Several minutes were still left in the boys high school basketball game, but the fan had been listening to the Carolina game on WPTF. He nudged a friend.

"Carolina is about to get beat!" he said. "The streak is going to be over."

Word spread quickly through the tiny gym. And then, while the two high school teams played on, the building began to empty.

"People started leaving the gym right at that moment," Woody Durham remembers. "They all went outside and got in their cars. The gym was in a residential part of town, so there were houses down the street behind the school, and there were cars parked up and down that road on both sides of the street. After that fan told everyone Carolina was about to lose, every single one of those cars had someone in it. You looked down that road and saw every car running and the windows starting to fog up from people sitting in the car listening to the radio. When that boys basketball game ended, I don't think there was anyone in [the gym] except the teams, the coaches, and the referees."

The Tar Heel players had no time to consider the enormity of the situation. They did not have the same reaction as Fleishman to McGuire's concession speech. Instead, they looked at each other incredulously. They had not spent endless afternoons and evenings in Woollen Gym running through McGuire's beloved "practicing with the clock" just to give up with two minutes left.

"They had us," Cunningham says. "I'm sure Coach was using psychology on us, but it really ticked us off, hearing him concede the game. We looked at each other, and there was a general consensus of, 'What the hell is he talking about?'"

With 12,000 fans screaming and thousands more back in North Carolina hunched over their radios, the impossible began. Kearns sank a basket that finally brought the Tar Heels even at 53–53 with 1:30 remaining. But Maryland still had an advantage: Millikan would simply instruct his team to hold the ball for the last shot.

That's exactly what they did, with precious seconds melting off the clock. The situation was clear—Maryland had no intention of allowing the Tar Heels another chance to touch the basketball. The Terrapins held Carolina's 16-game winning streak and national ranking in their hands. One of two things would happen: The Terps would make a shot and win the game, or they would miss and the game would go into overtime. In a less physical era, the situation greatly favored the offense. Any contact at all would result in potentially game-winning free throws.

With just seconds remaining, Maryland initiated its final play. Nick Davis, who would eventually be his squad's high scorer with 20 points, penetrated into the lane. Cunningham, who played one of his best defensive games in a season full of them, denied the pass to Terrapin star Bob O'Brien. That forced Davis to look for a second option. He dumped the ball inside to center Perry Moore, but Moore fumbled the ball out of bounds, and the final seconds ticked off the clock.

Overtime.

The extra session—Carolina's first since the win over South Carolina two months earlier—bore a striking resemblance to regulation, as the Tar Heels and Terrapins traded baskets. Once again, Maryland players held the ball for the final minute of the period, making sure that they would have the last opportunity to win the game. Once again, they missed; this time it was O'Brien whose last-second shot caromed off the back rim.

Double overtime.

Rosenbluth had been Carolina's offensive mainstay. The Tar Heels managed 12 points combined in the two overtimes—and he scored 8 of them. But tied at 61 with 3:30 to go, the Tar Heels turned not to Rosenbluth, but to Kearns. The feisty little point guard converted again, putting Carolina ahead 63–61.

Some observers thought McGuire's tendency to ride his starters would eventually hurt the Tar Heels late in close games. With no television timeouts to halt play, great stamina was required to hustle up and down the floor for the 35 to 38 minutes per game McGuire expected of his starters. The requirements were even tougher for a double-overtime game in front of a hostile crowd, but after almost 48 minutes of basketball, something strange began to happen: It was Maryland that began to wilt. The Terrapin offense couldn't find the range, and Carolina continued to hold the 2-point advantage.

With 1:09 remaining Rosenbluth fouled out with 25 points. But even his absence did not spark the Maryland offense, and Carolina eventually claimed an improbable 65–61 victory.

Rosenbluth was nonplussed. He looked at McGuire in the locker room and made a simple statement.

"Fifteen more to go, Coach."

"I wanted to choke him," McGuire remembered later.

The coach knew that 15 was the exact number of victories required to finish the regular season, ACC Tournament, and NCAA Tournament undefeated. He tried to quiet his star—the press would have loved to grab hold of Rosenbluth's bold predictions and use them to incite opponents—but the sharpshooter just laughed.

"I'm not really sure how we won that game," Cunningham says now. "But once we did, we were on a run. We felt like if Lennie wasn't having one of his big-time games, then Pete would have one. If Pete wasn't having one, Joe would have one, or Tommy would have one, or someone else would have one, and we would all help each other out."

Just like the victory over NC State, the win over Maryland sparked a unique celebration among Carolina fans (albeit without snow). The Tar Heels boarded the train immediately after the game and started the long trip back to North Carolina. One of the last stops on the line was Raleigh. They pulled into the station at 3:00 a.m. with most players barely awake. But their eyes snapped open wide when they spotted a large group of fans—mostly students—crowding around the platform to welcome them home.

○

The team had only four days to get ready for a home game against Duke. It would be Carolina's first game at Woollen Gym with the number one ranking, and demand for tickets was higher than for any basketball game in Tar Heel history. Woollen's capacity, which was listed at anywhere from 5,000 to 6,000 depending on the attentiveness of the fire marshal, limited the number of tickets available to students. School administrators had to come up with a rotating alphabetical ticketing system to accommodate demand. Students with last names in the first third of the alphabet would have the first opportunity for tickets to one game, students in the second third would get the first option for the next game, and the process would continue rotating for the rest of the season. Tickets for any one game rarely extended through the entire alphabet.

It took creativity to circumvent the standard procedures. Some students provided services—assistance with difficult academic projects or with lab work, for example—to peers whose last names were more favorable for particular games in exchange for their university ID cards.

The system was not ideal, and it angered some loyal fans who felt that they were being squeezed out by bandwagon jumpers. Rumors began sweeping the Carolina campus that a group of students who missed out on Duke tickets planned to force their way into the building for the game. The rumors became so pervasive that the University eventually had to enlist McGuire's help to quell the uprising. With the Saturday game just a few days away, the head coach and athletic director Chuck Erickson spoke through the *Daily Tar Heel*—under the headline McGuire Issues Appeal to Student Body—to request civil behavior outside Woollen Gym.

"We all regret that we do not have seating space for all the students and we can understand the disappointment of those who, under the priority system, will be unable to see the game," the head coach said. "On the other hand the authorities have worked it out the best way they could and the students should cooperate in good spirit."

McGuire was willing to lend his name to the effort, fully realizing that with his team's record at 17–0 and just seven games standing between the Tar Heels and a perfect regular season, students would do virtually anything he asked. He knew that he needed their support and was thrilled with the way basketball was beginning to take over the campus. But he also knew his team had enough distractions without worrying about a riot at the entrance.

The situation was more fuel for his crusade to obtain a better basketball facility in Chapel Hill. McGuire felt that promises made to him upon his hiring had gone unfulfilled. Now the University was reaping what it had sown—or failed to sow. With Reynolds the crown jewel of Tobacco Road basketball and Maryland playing in spacious Cole Field House, a groundswell was beginning for Carolina to build a similar facility. The logic seemed simple: The program had reached elite standards and needed an elite building. Word spread that the school could have sold upwards of 15,000 tickets for the Duke game. The combined factors of squeezed-out students and missed revenue had area writers echoing McGuire's calls for a new arena.

"Big time basketball in the form of Frank McGuire and his Yankee legions has come to Chapel Hill, and the University has not met the challenge," read a mid-February *Daily Tar Heel* editorial under the headline Needed: A New Palace for McGuire. "Fans sit on rickety

Lennie Rosenbluth soars for a rebound. His number 10 jersey is one of only eight retired in the history of the University of North Carolina basketball program.

One of four team photos taken during the 1956–57 season. The changing eligibility status of some players required multiple photos.

Above: Lennie Rosenbluth gives a stirring speech at the Carolina lettermen reunion in February 2004. Right: Rosenbluth and the spoils of victory at the 1956 Dixie Classic. Below, from left: Rosenbluth, Joe Quigg, Danny Lotz, Bob Cunningham, and Pete Brennan at the grand opening of the new Woollen Gym in October 2004.

Lennie Rosenbluth makes his way through the crowd after the 1957 championship game. He was named the most outstanding player of the NCAA Tournament.

Frank McGuire's New York–Chapel Hill recruiting pipeline paid dividends during his nine-season Carolina coaching career. All five starters on the 1957 title team had New York ties.

Sean May was intent on meeting Rosenbluth at the 2004
reunion. "To put up the numbers he did in just three
years is incredible," May said.

Two New Yorkers, Pete Brennan and Frank McGuire.
Brennan, one of the best players in Carolina history and
an honored jersey recipient, averaged a double-double for
his career and was a first-team All-American in 1958.

bleachers with no added luxury devices such as arm rests or backrests and consider themselves more than fortunate to be there."

Anyone who wanted to be there had to arrive early. Woollen was packed by 6:00 p.m. for the 8:00 p.m. tip-off against Duke. Any fans arriving less than two hours before the start of the game were turned away. As those unlucky few left, they might have encountered a strange sight—workers trying to wedge huge television cameras into a hole in a Woollen wall.

Any plan to televise a college basketball game was usually torpedoed by concerned radio executives. Yet the Carolina-Duke game was to mark the debut of a new broadcasting technique known as Broadvision. Sports coverage on television was still in its infancy— the World Series had been broadcast in color for the first time just 30 months earlier, in 1954, the same year that revenue for television broadcasters ($593 million) had eclipsed that of radio broadcasters for the first time. Baseball owners worried that television would be the end of their ticket revenues. Would anyone want to watch a game in person if it was available on TV? Some college athletics administrators asked the same question.

But Carolina had already sold every seat in Woollen Gymnasium, so there wasn't any ticket revenue to lose. At the time, public station Channel 4 was trying to build momentum in budding local television. UNC system president William Friday teamed with Billy Carmichael—a former ad executive—to brainstorm ways to harness some of television's potential.

Their solution combined the best of television and the best of radio. The plan for Broadvision was simple: air the video portion of the game on TV with no sound, so fans would be required to simultaneously tune in to the local audio broadcast of the game. WUNC committed to airing the Carolina-Duke game on February 9 and the Carolina–Wake Forest game four days later in the format. The upcoming rivalry clash with NC State on February 19 also seemed like a natural fit, but the Tuesday tip-off conflicted with numerous high school basketball games. Skittish after displays like the one witnessed by Woody Durham during the Maryland game, high school athletics officials persuaded WUNC not to air a game they felt would negatively impact prep basketball ticket sales.

"In view of the fine showing the Big Four teams are making again this year, particularly the first-place Tar Heels, we know there will be an unusual amount of interest in these games and we are particularly glad to be able to telecast them," said John Young, the assistant director of WUNC.

A generation of fans trained to "turn down the sound" was born. Broadvision made such an impact in Chapel Hill that even today, UNC operates an in-stadium radio frequency for basketball fans who feel compelled to listen to their radios while they watch the game in person.

The mechanics of implementing the new strategy were simple. The day of the Duke game, Carmichael and Friday armed themselves with steel chisels and enormous hammers. Their task was to chop a hole big enough for a camera lens in the Woollen Gymnasium wall.

"We spent that whole afternoon knocking a hole wide enough for the camera to be able to pan from goal to goal," Friday remembers. "Around 4:00 p.m., before the game started at 8:00, we finished making the room and carried great big cameras up there and got them into position."

Those cameras caught another incredible display in the long line of tremendous Duke-Carolina battles. Duke led by as many as 8 points in the first half and held a 41–36 halftime advantage. Carolina eventually battled back behind Rosenbluth's 35 points and appeared to have an insurmountable lead, 73–67, with less than a minute left. But the

Blue Devils began a frantic rally and took advantage of uncharacteristic Tar Heel sloppiness. They closed within 73–71 and then tied the score with just 24 seconds remaining.

It was yet another chance for Carolina to put its "practicing with the clock" plan into action. Rather than melt away the time, the Tar Heels attacked immediately. Kearns eventually drew a foul from Duke's Bobby Joe Harris with 16 seconds left. It seemed like a good play for the Devils—Kearns had missed his last five free throw attempts.

But he drilled these two, giving his team a 75–73 lead. Duke had plenty of time to tie the score, but a pair of last-second shots fell short, and Carolina advanced to 18–0.

Or, as Rosenbluth would remind his coach in the locker room, "Fourteen more."

With two straight last-possession victories, McGuire believed that his team's level of play had dropped since earlier in the season.

"The pressure has really gotten to us," he said. "If we went into the ACC tourney like we played tonight we'd get beaten on the first night. The boys look like they need a good rest."

There was no time for a good, long rest. A road game against Virginia was just two nights away. That would mean even more talk of winning streaks and championships.

"Duke is a good ball club," McGuire said immediately after the game. "We can never seem to catch them on an off night. This is the longest winning streak I've ever had and I hope it continues, but I don't want another one once this one is finished. It's too hard on the heart."

A win over Virginia on February 11, the 19th straight Carolina victory, did little to ease McGuire's stress. When the Tar Heels trailed the hapless Cavaliers—a team that would win just six games all season—30–26 at halftime, the hot-tempered head coach entered the locker room well ahead of his players and punched the dressing room door. Only manager Joel Fleishman saw the brief temper snap; McGuire's hand would be sore for two weeks.

The Tar Heels eventually managed a 68–59 win over the Cavaliers, thanks largely to 15 second-half points from Kearns. The triumph provided a brief moment of respite for McGuire—until he tried to go to sleep that night.

"I'm starting to have dreams about us losing," he said. "Not just losing, but getting killed. In the dream the score comes over the loudspeakers and it's some other team 106, Carolina nothing."

Wake Forest was intent on filling the role of "some other team." ACC scheduling was not yet an exact science, so the Tar Heels and Demon Deacons were set to square off twice in the ensuing 13 days, with a potential third meeting (the fourth of the season) coming one week later in the ACC Tournament.

The evening of February 13, the first of a three-game homestand for Carolina, got off to an inauspicious start when the lights at the entrance to Woollen began flickering. Another overflow crowd was scheduled to pack the venerable gym; as the fans filed in, they were swathed in partial darkness. Workers were dispatched to try to find replacement parts, but they encountered a problem—the lights used in Woollen were 20 years old, and no one knew where to find that model.

The Tar Heels almost suffered the same fate as their lights. Brennan went down with a sprained ankle in the first half and was limited throughout the second half. Despite losing one of its stars, however, Carolina got solid offensive contributions from defensive ace Cunningham. The pass-first guard scored 6 straight points late in the second half to stretch his team's lead to 68–57 with 3:36 remaining.

Just as in the Duke game, the lead proved hard to hold. Rosenbluth fouled out with 3:07 left, eliminating Carolina's primary offensive option and a reliable free throw shooter. Wake Forest applied defensive pressure all over the court and began to wreak havoc, forcing back-to-back turnovers and converting the turnovers into points. Playing in front of their home crowd, the Tar Heels were supposed to be the poised, veteran team. On the bench McGuire fiddled with his tie, pulling it tight against his collar.

Once again, though, Kearns provided a pardon. In what was becoming a routine pattern, he made two late free throws to stretch the lead back to 3 points, and the Tar Heels held on for a 72–69 victory. For McGuire, who had developed a healthy dislike of Wake Forest, the win was sweet.

"The boys were not as tight tonight as they were against Duke," he said. "And did you hear that crowd? Why, when we got ahead by 11, I thought it was New Year's Eve. It was great."

O

McGuire had come to Chapel Hill to raise the profile of basketball. He had succeeded, but he was finding that success had both its positives (like the great homecourt advantage against Wake Forest) and negatives. Everywhere he went, fans wanted to talk basketball.

"I almost hoped we could get beaten just to take the terrific pressure off the players," he said. "Well, not the players so much, because they kept cool even if I didn't. But the students and the alumni and the people generally were feeling the strain. Strangers would come up to me and slip me a nutmeg, a lucky coin, or a rabbit's foot to carry in my pocket, or a man might beg me to wear the same sports jacket to every game. Students were growing beards; they counted their steps from one class to another so they would take just the same number every day."

One student in particular believed that he had identified a lucky charm. That student was junior forward Pete Brennan, who had been given a car by his father during his sophomore year. The vehicle, a gray Chrysler, was in perilous condition due to several round-trip journeys to New York. It had no first gear, which meant Brennan usually tried to start it on a hill for smoother takeoff.

By the end of Brennan's sophomore year, the car rarely started, and he didn't have any money to fix it. So he put a sign on the driver's-side door—PLEASE DO NOT MOVE, AM GOING TO FIX UP IN SEPTEMBER—and signed his name, feeling sure that the effort was futile.

But when he returned to school for the start of his junior year, the car had not moved from its spot in front of the Monogram Club. Now wondering exactly how far he could push his luck, Brennan didn't move it for four more months. Parking tickets piled up on the windshield, but the Chrysler was never towed.

Finally, McGuire called Brennan into the basketball office.

"Pete, you've got to either move the car or have it towed, and I want it done right away," he said. "I'm tired of hearing about all these tickets."

At first Brennan acquiesced and turned to walk out of the office. But then he paused.

"Coach, I'll do whatever you want," he said. "But I think it's our good luck charm."

McGuire looked at his standout junior for a moment. This was risky—Brennan knew that his comment might incite the head coach's temper and provoke an explosion. McGuire picked up the phone and dialed a number.

It turned out to be the local police department on the other end of the line.

"Look," the son of a former New York City policeman said, "Brennan is going to leave the car there until the end of the basketball season."

It stayed immobile until the week of the February 19 NC State game. After McGuire placed his call to the police department, the car began to receive significant press. One of those stories, with an accompanying photo of Brennan perched on the fender, ran in the *Raleigh News & Observer*. The solution to breaking the Carolina stranglehold seemed obvious to State fans: move the car.

A group of enterprising students made the trip to Chapel Hill and pushed it down a hill. They had intentions of pushing it all the way out of town, but a group of trees blocked the way. As the crowning touch the Wolfpack operatives splashed bright red paint all over the previously gray exterior.

Once dawn broke, word of the mission spread quickly around Chapel Hill. Brennan found it slightly humorous, but his fellow students didn't share his outlook. With tip-off just a day away and a 20-game winning streak hanging in the balance, a group of UNC students rounded up a posse and went to retrieve the car. They pushed it back up the hill, put it exactly where it had rested before, and covered the red paint with Carolina blue paint.

"That car hadn't been painted in 20 years," Brennan recalls. "And then in the span of two days, it got two paint jobs."

Despite the best efforts of State fans, the attempt to provide the Wolfpack with some mojo did not work. Everett Case's team was on its way to its worst finish since the formation of the Atlantic Coast Conference—a meager 7–7 record in the league and just 15–11 overall. Carolina's trip to Reynolds as the favored team a month earlier had been big news; now State was seen as merely a prelude to the home finale against South Carolina three days later. The Gamecocks had taken the Tar Heels into overtime in their first meeting of the season, and it would be Rosenbluth's final home game. Already the demand for tickets was frenetic.

State still had some of the regal bearing befitting its place as the king of the league—reserves sat on the bench with two bright red blankets with "NC State" written in white—but the Wolfpack didn't have the talent to go with the reputation. They shot just 35 percent against Carolina while the Tar Heels made 50 percent of their field goals. The game was never in question, although McGuire took the opportunity—perhaps remembering 28- and 22-point losses to Case earlier in his Carolina career—to leave his starters in the game until two minutes remained. When McGuire finally removed them, his squad had a 28-point lead.

Asked about the extended use of his starters, McGuire looked shocked at the mere suggestion that he wanted to run up the score on the Wolfpack. "We hadn't played a game in nearly a week and the starters needed the work," he said.

The Tar Heels had time for just two practices before taking on South Carolina in the conclusion to the abbreviated home schedule. The Gamecocks were the quintessential one-man team, as hot-shooting Grady Wallace was on his way to the ACC scoring championship with an average of 31.2 points per game. He had bettered that average in the first contest against Carolina, notching 35 points.

The scoring explosion had embarrassed Cunningham, whose primary reputation was as a defensive stopper. Before one of the pre–South Carolina practices, he asked for an audience with McGuire.

"Coach, I want to guard Wallace," he said.

The head coach looked resigned to another scoring outburst. "Well, OK," he said. "You can play him. But I think he's too good for you, Bobby."

McGuire knew that one of his New York City boys would respond to that kind of challenge. As he went over the matchups on the chalkboard in the Woollen Gym locker room, he outlined a unique defensive strategy—four Tar Heels were going to play zone while

Cunningham guarded Wallace man-to-man. The coach assumed that the 6-foot-4 Wallace would get his points, but he didn't believe that the other South Carolina players were good enough to beat the Tar Heels. If Wallace could be held to around 25 points, the Gamecocks didn't have enough firepower to compete.

The game itself almost became secondary to the ceremonies attached to the last Chapel Hill game of the season. After three fantastic seasons at Carolina, it would be Lennie Rosenbluth's final home game. The overflow crowd of 6,000 began arriving at 5:00 p.m. for the 8:00 p.m. tip-off and filled the bleachers more than two hours before the scheduled start. Minutes before tip, the Tar Heels entered the gym to the usual home accompaniment of "Sweet Georgia Brown." After proceeding through a layup line, all the players except Rosenbluth went to the sideline. Three years of varsity memories washed over him.

Despite the year of prep school, he had arrived at Carolina still naïve about the ways of the South. One of the first things he had noticed on campus was the fact that seemingly everyone he met had three names: Ida Mae Jones. Billy Ray Johnson. Becky Ann Walters. Back home, two names usually sufficed. He had never been anything other than Lennie Rosenbluth. After a few days in his new town, however, he altered that. He began to introduce himself as Lennie Shoota-lot Rosenbluth.

Plenty of those shots found the net, and his number 10 jersey would eventually be retired by the University, one of only eight such honors given in the illustrious history of Carolina basketball. As of 2011 Rosenbluth still holds Carolina's single-season scoring average record (28.0 points per game in 1956–57) and career average scoring record (26.9 points per game), without the benefit of the three-point shot. His 2,045 career points, compiled in only three seasons due to his freshman ineligibility, were a school record for 21 years and currently rank fourth behind four-year players Tyler Hansbrough, Phil Ford, and Sam Perkins.

When Rosenbluth's name was announced over the Woollen Gym public-address system, the cheering was long and loud. The standing ovation lasted for three minutes, all while Rosenbluth sheepishly looked around the gym and lifted his hand to acknowledge the fans. Student body president Bob Young (no relation to the Bob Young on the basketball team) took the microphone and presented Rosenbluth with an engraved trophy.

Then the real drama began.

Quigg was battling a virus and had to sit out the first half. Although Cunningham, aided by quality help from Brennan, harassed Wallace all over the court, other Gamecocks found offensive success. Buoyed by those unexpected contributions, they edged out to a 37–35 halftime lead.

The Tar Heels had looked tight in the first 20 minutes. The pre-game ceremony for Rosenbluth and planned postgame festivities to honor McGuire seemed to have taken their minds off basketball. A loss would mean very little overall—Carolina had already clinched the ACC regular-season championship and the top seed in the conference tournament. Moreover, dreams of a national championship were still somewhat foreign; Kansas had the big guy named Wilt, after all. But everyone wanted to do what even Case had been unable to do: cruise through an ACC season undefeated.

The jitters were gone in the second half. In their place was the conference powerhouse everyone had expected. Carolina immediately retook the lead and settled down en route to a 75–62 victory. When Wallace checked out of the game, he had contributed just 11 points. Before leaving the floor he grabbed the hands of Brennan and Cunningham, who had combined to make him virtually invisible most of the night. "That's the best defense anyone has ever played against me," he said. The Woollen Gym crowd gave him a rousing ovation. It was the perfect illustration of how McGuire wanted a home game to happen: his team emerging with a victory and an overflow crowd maintaining respect for the opponent.

The coach lavished praise on Cunningham after the game, calling his performance "one of the greatest man-to-man defensive exhibitions I've ever seen." But most of the postgame talk was not about Cunningham's defense or Rosenbluth's final game. Instead, it was about yet another ceremony, this time for the head coach.

Local travel agency owner George Hogan and gas station proprietor Obie Davis had spearheaded a campaign to purchase a car for McGuire. Not just any car, but a Cadillac. They had solicited donations from across the community (students were not permitted to contribute more than $1 apiece).

The automobile would not be a surprise to McGuire, as news of the planned purchase had been in the newspapers for almost a month. But the pomp surrounding the event was overwhelming even to a native New Yorker. Carlisle Higgins, associate justice of the North Carolina Supreme Court, emceed the event, grabbing the microphone and lavishing praise on the 22–0 Tar Heels and their coaches. Freshman coach Vince Grimaldi and assistant coach Buck Freeman were given small gifts (Freeman received a portable television set and a transatlantic radio) as tokens of the crowd's appreciation. Then McGuire, with his wife and two daughters at his side, was called to center court. There he was presented with a set of car keys and told to exit Woollen Gym to see his new automobile.

When the family went outside, they found a shiny blue-and-white Cadillac that cost approximately $4,500—more than one-third of McGuire's annual pay from UNC. The coach, for one of the few times in his life, was rendered virtually speechless.

"I've always watched people receive those big prizes on television but I never figured it would happen to a coach," he said.

His team, of course, found great humor in the ceremony. The coach occasionally let Brennan and Cunningham drive his old DeSoto station wagon to his Candlewood Lake vacation home in upstate New York. It was a reward for the players and a valuable service for McGuire, as he could fly his family to the lake and arrive with a car waiting. The chosen chauffeurs, meanwhile, would be close to their New York homes and could hitchhike from Candlewood Lake to see their parents. Cunningham's father was a steel mill worker, and Brennan's father worked three jobs (including stints as a milkman and subway conductor) to support his family. There was no money for plane tickets home, so McGuire's generosity was appreciated.

The plan usually went off without a hitch. But on one trip Brennan and Cunningham failed to heed the coach's warnings to keep close track of the oil level. About four hours outside of Chapel Hill, the DeSoto sputtered and produced a loud pop, and smoke began billowing out of the back. Stranded and unfamiliar with cars, the two players looked at each other.

"What was that last thing Coach told us to watch out for?" Brennan asked his teammate.

"I think it's the oil," Cunningham said.

The best plan of action seemed obvious to Brennan. He fixed Cunningham, his Sigma Nu fraternity brother, with a serious stare.

"Bobby, you better call Coach and tell him what happened," he said.

Both knew that it would not be a pleasant call. It was one thing to miss a layup or fail to box out. It was quite another to blow the head coach's engine on the side of the road in Virginia. Finally, they made the sheepish call.

"He let us have it," Cunningham recalls. "He really chewed us out."

Before the South Carolina game, already aware of the impending ceremony, the players had begged their head coach for a ride down Franklin Street in the shiny new vehicle. After a couple of weeks, McGuire did finally relent, but as the team gazed at the shiny blue exterior and pristine white interior on February 22, that possibility seemed like a long shot. Cunningham nudged Brennan.

"Pete," he said, "there's no way he's going to let us drive that car to New York."

Chapter 9
Road Tested

With two games left in the regular season, Frank McGuire hardly needed extra reasons to be concerned about his squad. The buzz about an undefeated season was becoming overwhelming. Everywhere the coach went, he was asked about the possibility. His team, which had occupied the back page of the newspaper for most of the first two months of the season, was suddenly front-page news even when they didn't play a game. McGuire, who liked eating out, also found that every restaurant in Chapel Hill was suddenly populated with basketball experts. His late-night strategy sessions at home with Buck Freeman increased in frequency and intensity. The head coach continued to express the opinion that a loss would be good for his team. There was beginning to be more talk about the broad idea of an undefeated season than the specific task of winning individual games.

It looked like he might get his wish in the February 26 game at Wake Forest. Joe Quigg had been limited in the previous contest against South Carolina and was taken to the infirmary with the flu immediately after the victory. That was where he remained when the Carolina team bus left for Winston-Salem at 2:00 p.m. on February 25. McGuire wanted to put his team through a workout at Memorial Coliseum, where they had never played. The Baptist school had made the unique decision in 1946 to relocate the campus from Wake Forest—about half an hour from Raleigh—to Winston. School trustees and alums battled over the decision for a decade, but the move was finally completed in 1956.

Although it might have been a controversial decision at Wake, it was not mourned at Carolina. The first time the Brennan/Quigg/Kearns/Cunningham class had played in Gore Gym in Wake Forest, they were greeted with a large banner that read WELCOME BROOKLYN CATHOLICS. Most of the New York natives had played in hostile environments before, but those were usually bandboxes that could accommodate no more than a couple hundred fans. Although tiny by today's standards, Gore Gym was 10 times bigger than what most players had seen before.

As freshmen the touted recruiting class had heard stories about Gore. On the bus ride to their first game there, they discussed the need to remain blasé in the face of what was certain to be some unfriendly commentary from the fans.

"I was determined not to change my expression," Pete Brennan recalls. "No matter what happened—good, bad, or indifferent—I wanted to keep the exact same expression on my face."

That expression evidently made quite an impression on the Wake fans. As the Tar Babies—the 1955 nickname for the Carolina freshman team—went through their warm-up drills, the heckling began. Brennan was tagged with the nickname "Sad Sack," in reference to a popular comic book character that was about to be made into a live-action film starring Jerry Lewis. Opposing fans would continue to call him Sad Sack throughout his Tar Heel career.

But Brennan didn't frown. The Tar Babies eventually pulled out a victory in that game, and the team celebrated on the bus while waiting for the final stragglers to board. Suddenly, they heard sharp pings and clunks. Wake fans were pelting the bus with rocks.

Two years later, in front of a sellout crowd of more than 8,200 that promised to be even more hostile than usual, McGuire knew that the undefeated season might be nearing its end. Without Quigg, Lennie Rosenbluth's contributions would be even more important. But as the team assembled in the Memorial Coliseum locker room hours before the game, Rosenbluth's playing status was uncertain.

The All-American was huddled in a corner, nursing a severe cough. McGuire tried to ignore the hacking and address his players. He wrote the matchups on the chalkboard and began to describe exactly how he wanted his team to attack the 13th-ranked Demon Deacons. Rosenbluth continued to cough loudly, however, and finally McGuire could ignore it no longer. He whirled and faced his star.

"Lennie, that is the worst cough I have ever heard. You're obviously dying. I don't want you to die any place but Chapel Hill. Get dressed, Lennie, and we'll call off the game and drive you home."

Rosenbluth's teammates tried to hide smirks. McGuire walked over and draped an arm over Rosenbluth's shoulder.

"My boy, I can't promise you that you will live to see the old school again, but I do promise that you'll have the finest three-day Irish wake in the history of North Carolina."

By this point the other players in the room could not hide their laughter. Everyone chuckled, and eventually Rosenbluth—who declined the offer to go back to Chapel Hill and join Quigg in the infirmary—laughed also.

Based on the electricity in the room, McGuire judged that his team was ready. Other than the blowout of NC State, they hadn't played particularly well lately, but he knew that Wake Forest got Carolina's blood boiling. In fact, Wake got his blood boiling, too. McGuire would later dismiss the value of pregame pep talks in his first book, *Offensive Basketball:* "I do not believe in pre-game pep talks," he wrote. "It is detrimental to push your team to a high emotional point too often during the season. The morale of winning teams is consistent and they do not require the emotional approach."

He was in the process of coaching the ultimate winning team. But on this occasion he broke his own rule. Realizing that the Memorial Gymnasium locker room walls were paper thin and that the Deacons were sitting on the other side of the wall—where he was certain they could hear everything going on in the Carolina locker room—McGuire began one of his greatest dramatic performances as the Tar Heel head coach.

He went back to the chalkboard to discuss the matchups again. But then he appeared to get sidetracked by the thought of Wake assistant Bones McKinney, a former Carolina player who was an assistant in name only. Murray Greason was the school's head coach but had already turned over many of the coaching duties to McKinney.

"I'll never forget it," Kearns says. "Frank is doing the matchups on the board and he just starts railing on Wake Forest and McKinney. He was really getting after them. He was raising his voice and talking about how they were these son-of-a-bitch Baptists who hated we Catholics and didn't respect us and hated our mothers and everything else. It was priceless."

The teams had more than just cultural differences. Their styles of play were also very distinct. Carolina preferred to play the New York way, with a free-flowing offense and a fast-paced tempo. Wake was much more structured, wanting to control the clock and keep the score under 70.

Wake succeeded in that endeavor. The Deacons rolled out to a 47–39 lead in the second half. With under a minute to play, they were still clinging to a 64–63 lead. Without Quigg the Carolina offense had been dependent almost entirely on Rosenbluth, who was on his way to a 30-point performance despite the supposedly crippling cough. (McGuire would later note that he never saw Rosenbluth cough on the court during the game.)

Rosenbluth hit two free throws with 46 seconds left to give Carolina a 65–64 advantage. Wake Forest still had a chance to make the game-winning shot. All 8,200 fans, each of whom had paid the seemingly exorbitant price of $2 per ticket, were on their feet. It looked like the end of the undefeated season. But then defensive wizard Cunningham came up with a steal. He passed ahead to Brennan, who was fouled. With Quigg listening to his teammates on the radio and agonizing over the final seconds, Brennan made one of two free throws, and the Carolina lead grew to 66–64.

Still, Wake had a chance to tie. But a missed shot landed in the hands of Tommy Kearns, who completed a three-point play at the buzzer to provide the final winning margin of 69–64.

Carolina returned to the locker room a spent team. Winning every game, it turned out, was exhausting.

"You know, I was kissing that one goodbye for a while there," McGuire said. "Bobby Cunningham is the unsung hero of our ball club."

Only one game stood between Carolina and an undefeated regular season: a road trip to Duke. Through 1954, when Carolina's final regular-season opponent was The Citadel, that last slot had rotated among different teams. But beginning in 1955, the athletic directors at the two rival schools made it a priority to establish Carolina-Duke as the final game of the regular season. (Today, that is always the case.)

The Blue Devils were a respectable 8–5 in the conference—they boasted a better league record than either Wake Forest or NC State and were tied with Maryland—and 13–10 overall. They had the advantage of playing in Duke Indoor Stadium, where Carolina had not won since 1950. Duke was 8–0 in its home building during the season, a record that included wins over Wake and Maryland, two teams that had already given Carolina fits. Although Quigg was finally out of the infirmary and would make the trip to Durham, he was still feeling weak and was cleared for only limited action.

The capacity at Duke Indoor was 9,000, and it was full well before the 8:15 p.m. tip-off. Although his team appeared to have the talent to play with the Tar Heels—the matchup in Chapel Hill a month earlier had been just a 2-point game—Duke head coach Hal Bradley decided to employ a physical, bruising style of play designed to knock Carolina off its rhythm.

Rather than slowing down Carolina, the roughhouse tactics seemed to disrupt Duke's game. Carolina moved out to a comfortable 47–34 halftime advantage.

But surging in front of their overflow crowd, Duke came all the way back, eventually gaining the lead with less than five minutes to play. The physicality of the game took its toll: Cunningham had fouled out with 14 minutes still left in the second half, and all five Blue Devil starters followed. As soon as that happened, the Tar Heels retook control of the game. Rosenbluth finished with 40 points, just the fifth 40-point performance in Carolina basketball history (he accounted for three of the other four as well). His team stretched the margin of victory to 86–72 and claimed a perfect 24–0 regular season.

McGuire was reveling in the achievement as the team boarded the bus. Sophomore Gehrmann Holland caught his attention.

"Hey, Coach," Holland said. "How come I didn't play more?" A seldom-used 6-foot-3 guard described as "hefty" in Carolina's postseason media guide, Holland thought he had deserved more floor time in a game that was out of hand in the final minutes.

McGuire disagreed. Vocally.

"What the hell do you mean you should've played more?" he thundered. "We just went 24–0 and now you want to complain about playing time? Get out of here."

Holland remained, frozen. All the players had seen McGuire's temper explode, so it wasn't clear if he was just blowing off steam or literally wanted Holland off the bus.

It turned out it was the latter.

"Get out!" he screamed. Holland complied and hitchhiked back to Chapel Hill.

He missed an eventful bus ride. As the team was preparing to depart, they noticed a large group of Duke students surrounding the bus. That wasn't particularly unusual. Outside of the Chapel Hill campus, where McGuire was very specific in demanding good sportsmanship from the fans, it was fairly common practice to harass opponents on their way in and out of town.

As the bus began to shake, however, it became clear that this was more than just a typical attempt at intimidation.

"We really thought they were going to tip it over," Cunningham recalls. "It was really nasty. If they would have had a Molotov cocktail to throw at us, I think they would have done it."

McGuire's bunch of feisty New Yorkers didn't plan to sit idly and wait to be toppled. The head coach, as usual, was seated at the front of the bus, and a few players filed up the aisle on their way to an intended meeting with the offending fans.

"Let us off of here, Coach," they said. "We're going to go kick their ass."

The coach knew better. They were badly outnumbered and had much more to risk than a bunch of overconfident students did.

McGuire had some players—Quigg among them—who probably would do a considerable amount of damage to the average scrawny college student. But a brawl would draw attention from the ACC office and potentially result in suspensions for the conference tournament. There was too much to lose.

"Stay on the bus," he said firmly.

"Coach, we're not going to take this," Cunningham said.

McGuire fixed him with his most stern glare.

"Stay. On. The. Bus."

His players stayed on the bus, and it pulled away within moments, having never been toppled. As they drove, the head coach knew there was only one atmosphere that was more of a cauldron of heated emotion than the Duke crowd they had just encountered.

The ACC Tournament.

Chapter 10

The Foul
That Saved
a Season

The ACC Tournament was the most-hated, best-loved event in all of college basketball.

Atlantic Coast Conference head basketball coaches despised it. Their teams finished playing a 14-game, double round-robin schedule to determine a regular-season champion. But that championship came with little more than a nod of the head and a smile, because only the tournament champion received the league's automatic berth into the NCAA Tournament. Only one representative from each league could participate, so a misstep in the ACC Tournament meant an otherwise superior team would see its season end.

For McGuire and his 24–0 team, this was an especially troubling prospect. They had established their dominance during the regular season. But the way the brackets shaped up—Duke–South Carolina and Maryland-Virginia in the afternoon sessions, Carolina-Clemson and State-Wake in the evening quarterfinals—the Tar Heels would likely have to beat Wake and either Maryland or Duke just to earn a spot in the NCAA Tournament. All three of those teams had come within a possession of beating Carolina within the past month.

"The way it is now, these regular season games mean nothing," McGuire said. "We're just providing entertainment for the students. I told my boys before we played NC State in Raleigh this year, 'Don't worry, this game means little.' Why did I say that? Because the regular season games in this conference are meaningless. You tell coaches from other parts of the country that and they don't believe you. Why should anyone play 14 league games, 2 against each conference member, that will be junked at the season's end?

"State has 17 games (in Reynolds Coliseum) before the tournament and that is a tremendous advantage. I don't think it will be long before you see a change."

The change McGuire wanted was naming the regular-season champion the official conference champion. Several other leagues, including the Big Seven, already followed that practice. Kansas had dropped another conference game on February 21, losing 56–54 to Oklahoma State in Stillwater, but the Jayhawks won the regular-season championship and received an automatic bid into the NCAA Tournament.

When a midseason vote of coaches was taken, seven of the ACC's eight head basketball coaches voted to change the method of determining the conference champion. The lone holdout?

Not surprisingly, it was Everett Case. The North Carolina State leader had spent enough time in Indiana high school hoops to fall in love with tournament basketball. He loved the format of bringing every school together in the same venue, loved the unpredictability, loved the publicity it generated, and loved the pressure. Of course, it helped that he usually had the best team, which gave him a better way to deal with the pressure than some of his coaching companions.

Contrary to popular belief, however, Case did not create the ACC Tournament. Something similar existed as early as 1922 in the unwieldy Southern Conference, which had 17 teams and essentially went to a tournament out of necessity. From 1932 to 1950 the event was usually held at tiny Memorial Auditorium in Raleigh. When it moved to Reynolds Coliseum in 1951, it began to gain popularity in proportion to the significant increase in seating capacity. The ACC continued the Southern Conference tradition largely out of force of habit. Much of that first league season in 1954 was run on a trial-and-error basis, the tournament included. If it had flopped, it probably would have met its end. Instead, it thrived and became an essential part of the ACC culture.

The Tar Heels had experienced very little success in the event—either in its early incarnation as the Southern Conference Tournament or more recently in the ACC Tournament. Their last postseason championship had come more than a decade previous, in 1945, and they had not even been a finalist since 1947.

Considering that an ACC championship was a prerequisite for continuing the miracle 1956–57 season, this qualified as a disturbing trend. But McGuire didn't believe that his teams were somehow unprepared for tournament competition. After all, he had experienced success in the postseason at St. John's. Instead, he believed he simply didn't have the right amount of talent to compete with powerhouse conference opponents.

There has not been a public sale of ACC Tournament tickets since 1966, but in 1957 it was still possible for average fans (including Woody Durham, who attended his first ACC Tournament that year) to secure tickets. The event ran from Thursday through Saturday, which meant Wake County schools usually had a rash of unexplained absences the first two days of the tournament. The routine for fans on quarterfinal Thursday was fairly standard: attend the afternoon session, dash out for dinner (often at the S&W Cafeteria), and then return for the evening session.

Carolina's players were less intrigued than their followers by the event.

"You have to realize that none of us had any relatives who went to games," Joe Quigg says. "We had no one here. No mother, no father, nothing. So everyone assumed we couldn't wait for the ACC Tournament because it would be in a big arena with lots of tickets, but that wasn't the case."

Players often gave their tickets to student managers, who would then attempt to sell the entire weekend's passes.

The Tar Heels made sure they would hang around for the Friday semifinals with an 81–61 win over hapless Clemson. Rosenbluth poured in 45 points, the second time he had hit that figure against the Tigers. There was little time to celebrate his achievement. As expected, Wake Forest dispatched NC State in the 9:00 p.m. game, setting up the fourth Carolina-Wake meeting of the year on Friday.

The "$60,000 slot machine," as one skeptical coach had called the ACC Tournament, was about to produce one of its most memorable games.

O

Bones McKinney, the de facto Wake Forest coach, decided he needed to try something different for the semifinal meeting with Carolina. One of the problems with playing a team four times was trying to find a strategy that the other team hadn't already seen. McKinney had something special in mind for the Tar Heels.

But he also maintained a healthy sense of paranoia regarding his alma mater. With less than 24 hours before the game, there was not enough time to bus his team back to Winston for a practice. The old

Wake Forest campus and familiar Gore Gym, on the other hand, were just minutes away from Raleigh.

On Friday morning he loaded his squad onto a bus and headed for Gore. Wake played zone on occasion, a suitable defense for a team that did not have the individual raw talent possessed by Carolina. But McKinney wanted to give the Heels a new look, so he created a variation of the one-three-one zone called the Fruit Salad Defense. The plan was simple: stop Rosenbluth and—the constant goal of Wake against Carolina—slow the tempo. It would put more pressure on the Tar Heels' ballhandlers and, in theory, provide Wake with the early advantage of surprise, which might be too much to overcome in what was expected to be a tight game. At minimum it would allow the Deacons to build an early lead and seize momentum.

Imagine McKinney's surprise when Carolina began the semifinal with a three-guard lineup that included the seldom-used Ken Rosemond. Later, McKinney would claim that he had spotted a suspicious-looking janitor at Gore Gym and accuse the janitor of being a Tar Heel spy employed by McGuire to spirit information to the enemy. Instead of providing an early-game boost, the Fruit Salad Defense was picked apart by the Tar Heels as the top-seeded team in the tournament jumped to an early 10–0 lead.

But Wake Forest was too good to suffer a blowout, especially with a chance to end Carolina's magical season. The players were talented, certainly, but they had something else motivating them: a deep dislike for anything related to Carolina.

"People want to know sometimes how we were able to play so well against them with them having better material than us," Wake's Jackie Murdock says. "My answer most of the time has been pretty simple: hate. I don't hate them now, but when we were playing it was hate. And I think they felt that same way about us, too."

Whether it was hatred or pride (or a combination thereof), something propelled Wake back into the game. The Deacons closed to within 33–29 at halftime, setting the stage for one of the most controversial finishes in ACC Tournament history.

McGuire frequently pointed out that the familiarity created by multiple regular-season matchups made it exceptionally difficult to beat a team again in the ACC Tournament. That was one of the many reasons why he wanted to eliminate the event. But that same familiarity also created an undeniably tense atmosphere that fans loved. The final minutes against Wake were just such a fan-friendly situation. The teams battled equally throughout the second half, with neither able to gain a sizable advantage. With little time remaining and Wake holding a 1-point lead, Pete Brennan went to the free throw line. As he toed the line, he heard McKinney yelling, "Don't choke up, Brennan!"

The unflappable forward nailed both charity tosses. Then he turned to the Wake bench and shouted, "How's that for choking, Bones?"

Wake's Jim Gilley, who had been at the center of a Wake-Carolina brawl earlier in the season, made a pair of free throws on the next possession to give his team a 59–58 lead with 55 seconds remaining. McKinney signaled for a switch from man-to-man defense to zone. But not everyone saw the signal. Gilley thought his team was still in man-to-man and reacted accordingly. Holes opened in the Wake Forest defense. Seconds ticked off the clock, one at a time.

The noise inside Reynolds Coliseum reflected the unusual mix of anticipation, excitement, and fear found only at nail-biting sporting events. Many of the fans in attendance had superstitious ticks—even famous fans like Kay Kyser, who had led the Kay Kyser Orchestra in the 1940s and then retired to North Carolina. A close friend of McGuire, Kyser enjoyed Tar Heel basketball, but he saw very few games during the run to the 1957 championship. He became convinced that it was bad luck for him to watch a game in person. So during the semifinal game against Wake Forest, the former radio star sat in his car, waiting for someone to tell him that the game was over and to describe the thrilling final minutes.

McGuire had not drawn up a complex plan for his team's potential game-winner. Players liked to say that the squad had only two set offensive plays, and both of those were inbounds plays designed to create an open shot in situations where Carolina needed a basket very quickly.

This was not that kind of situation. So McGuire went with the play that had gotten him to 25–0. He looked at Buck Freeman and then at his team huddled around him as the din rose in Reynolds.

"Get the ball to Lennie," he said.

That's exactly what his team did. With about 50 seconds left, Rosenbluth received a pass near the foul line. He drove across the lane and tossed up a sweeping hook shot. Deacon reserve Wendell Carr tried to defend the play and collided with Rosenbluth. As the ball trickled through the net, official Jim Mills blew his whistle.

Every eye in the building turned to Mills. If he called a blocking foul, Carolina would have a chance to clinch the game with a three-point play. If he called a charging foul, it might mean the end of the Tar Heels' dream season.

"I thought it was a charge," Murdock says. "All the Wake Forest people thought it was a charge."

Rosenbluth remembers it differently: "He fouled me. I knew he had fouled me."

Mills agreed with Rosenbluth. He signaled a blocking foul and counted the basket. Carolina led 60–59. McGuire called a timeout before his star could attempt the free throw.

"Lennie, just make this shot," McGuire told him. "When you do that, we'll be 2 points ahead and all they can do in regulation is tie the game."

Rosenbluth stepped to the line and dropped through his free throw for a 61–59 lead. The play seemed to soak every last ounce of energy out of Wake Forest, and the Deacons failed to tie the game in the closing seconds. The usually talkative McKinney declined to speak to reporters after the game, as did the four Wake Forest co-captains.

A shaky McGuire, just minutes removed from a potentially devastating loss, was candid with the media.

"I couldn't even write my name on the way down here," he said after arriving at the interview location. "A kid asked me for an autograph and I couldn't even write my name."

O

There was some concern about a letdown after Carolina's heart-pounding win over its Big Four rival. The memory of the tight overtime win in Columbia still lingered, and on this Friday night, the Tar Heels had been only 50 seconds from the end of their season. Even the epic win over Wake would not salvage the season if the team fell short of the ACC championship and, by extension, a bid to the NCAA Tournament.

The sixth-seeded Gamecocks, a team that had finished 5–9 in the ACC during the regular season, squeaked by Duke in the quarterfinals and then edged Maryland in the semifinals. Simply advancing to the championship game was an achievement for them; like the Tar Heels, they had never stayed alive until the final game before. In fact, the 1957 ACC Tournament championship game was the first ever that did not involve two Big Four teams.

South Carolina's magical run came to an abrupt end. Rather than being content with their win over Wake, the Tar Heels built on that victory and breezed to the ACC title with a 95–75 triumph over the Gamecocks. The most valuable player of the tournament was, of course, Rosenbluth, who outscored South Carolina's touted Grady Wallace 38–28 in the tournament final. (Rosenbluth was the first Carolina player to win the MVP award and would remain the only one for another nine years.) In addition to making one of the most remembered shots in tournament history, Rosenbluth averaged 35.3 points and 9.3 rebounds over the weekend and shot nearly 60 percent from the field. His 106 tournament points set a new league record. Brennan joined him on the All-Tournament team after scoring 22 points in the championship game; Kearns, Quigg, and Cunningham all made the second team.

The Tar Heels had no time to enjoy these honors. Regional seeding was still used at this time, so every team stayed in its natural region to minimize expensive travel, especially on such short notice. The ACC champion had a predetermined foe in the opening round—the Ivy League champion. In just three days the Tar Heels would take on Yale.

The predetermined game site made the need for speedy travel arrangements palatable. To begin its quest for the 1957 national championship, Carolina would go to a place only slightly less familiar to most of the roster than Woollen Gym: Madison Square Garden.

Chapter 11

Cops, Robbers, and the Garden

Almost every player on the North Carolina roster was familiar with the type of triple-header that unfolded on March 12 at Madison Square Garden. Six teams assembled at the basketball mecca for first-round NCAA action. The first game matched Syracuse and Connecticut, the second pitted Canisius against West Virginia, and the nightcap featured the marquee pairing of Carolina and Yale. It was the kind of event that the New Yorkers on the Tar Heel roster might have tried to gain access to as youngsters, either by sneaking in one of the back Garden entrances or securing tickets from a recruiter. Now they didn't need tickets. They were the main attraction.

"It was such a thrill to play in the Garden for a second time that season," Bob Cunningham says. "You have to remember, to play in front of your family was still a very big deal. They weren't watching all

141

our games on television. They weren't traveling to our games in Chapel Hill. I was the first kid in my family to go to college, and my dad was working such long hours when I was in high school that he didn't even get to see a lot of those games. So to see me in college playing for an undefeated team was a big thrill for him.

"And it wasn't just your family that wanted to come. Everyone from the neighborhood wanted to come see you play. You started to realize you had friends you had never seen before."

Even Frank McGuire had ticket problems. He called an acquaintance at the Garden office and requested 60 tickets, 30 on one side of the arena and 30 on the other. The box office manager had to be consulted. The answer was polite but firm: The Garden could provide 60 tickets, but they would have to be on the same side of the arena.

McGuire was equally polite but firm. That arrangement simply would not work. He needed 30 on one side and 30 on the other. Perplexed, the ticket manager probed the unusual request. Wouldn't the Carolina coach want all his friends to sit together?

"You're right, they're all for my friends," replied McGuire, the son of a police officer. "But half of my friends are cops and half of my friends are robbers, and I can't have the cops and robbers sitting on the same side."

Faced with that sort of ironclad logic, there was only one solution: McGuire received his tickets split into two groups of 30.

Based on a map, North Carolina was the farthest flung of any of the participants. But the Tar Heel team was probably the best fit in terms of panache. As usual, McGuire instructed his boys to look spotless when they arrived in New York. They were dressed in their normal travel gear: Carolina blue blazers with a UNC patch, gray flannel slacks, and polished black tassel loafers. Some wore coats over the ensemble—always 100-percent-wool overcoats, sometimes accented with a gray scarf. Very few members of the team came from families with any sort of wealth, but when they walked into Madison Square Garden, they looked every bit as upper crust as Ivy League Yale. Each player hefted a large dark blue travel bag with a UNC logo; rather than look bulky, it seemed to add to the appearance of a businessman preparing to preside over a meeting.

The team uniforms were equally impressive to style-conscious New Yorkers. The Tar Heels took the floor in their shiny warm-up uniforms—fittingly, the home whites—and immediately looked comfortable in the big city. Theirs was one of the few squads in the nation to wear high white socks (marked with Carolina blue stripes) rather than ankle-huggers. It was another distinctive touch for a distinctive team.

The Tar Heels liked to think of themselves as playing Eastern basketball in a Southern location. But grouped with five true Eastern teams, the differences immediately became obvious. Canisius and Syracuse, the potential next two opponents in the NCAA Tournament, played a bruising style of basketball. Despite a sizable height disadvantage (the Bulldogs gave up at least 3 inches at every position), Yale followed a similar game plan and tried to club Carolina into submission.

The crowd buzzed when the score was tied at 40 at halftime. It was an educated group of spectators; they knew the history of Everett Case's NC State teams rolling up impressive regular-season records only to falter in the NCAA Tournament. For that reason most fans were naturally suspicious of Atlantic Coast Conference basketball teams. Popular wisdom suggested that members of that conference simply didn't have the pedigree to compete with the true national basketball powers like the University of San Francisco or the University of Kentucky.

That theory appeared solid when Carolina led just 62–60 with 10 minutes remaining. Rosenbluth would lead his team with 29 points, but it was an unlikely shooting performance by Cunningham—who finished with 12 points, almost all of them in the final 10 minutes of the game—that eventually stretched Carolina's lead. Employing only six players to Yale's nine, McGuire's Tar Heels finally claimed a 90–74 victory.

A mere three days later, Carolina's tour of the East Coast continued with a regional semifinal game in Philadelphia, against Canisius. On the morning of the big game, basketball news was bumped down the front page of the *Daily Tar Heel* by breaking news. A banner headline read RAID RULES ORDER OF THE DAY. The UNC Student Council had issued a stern warning: "Active attendance or participation of any sort in a panty raid is very definitely a violation of gentlemanly conduct and thus a violation of the Campus Code. A participant of a recent caper has been placed on probation for such a violation."

McGuire was probably thankful his team was removed from such roguish shenanigans. In the span of a week, Carolina had traveled to Reynolds Coliseum, Madison Square Garden, and Philadelphia's Palestra, three of the era's signature arenas in college basketball. Canisius came with impressive references—this was the team that had eliminated the Wolfpack the previous year—but without the pressure of having local family and friends in attendance, the Tar Heels played a much more effective game than they had in New York. Carolina jumped to a 39–25 halftime lead, and Rosenbluth poured in 39 points to set the Palestra record for points by a visiting player. The game was never in question as UNC clinched an 87–75 victory.

There was little time to prepare for the next day's Eastern Regional championship game. McGuire had assigned Buck Freeman to scout eventual opponent Syracuse; Freeman reported that the team loved to push the ball up the court and likely would try to play a physical brand of defense. As usual, Freeman's evaluation was accurate. The Tar Heels shot 45 free throws and converted 33 of them. They raced to a 37–28 halftime advantage and held the lead throughout the second half. The

67–58 win temporarily gave Carolina a new college basketball record: 30–0 overall. The previous record for wins in an undefeated season had been the 29–0 mark posted by the University of San Francisco in 1956. As McGuire quickly pointed out, one Carolina loss would hand the record right back to the Dons.

Most experts had assumed that Carolina's national semifinal contest would be against Adolph Rupp and his powerful Kentucky squad, which had spent much of the year in the nation's top five. But Michigan State, which had narrowly escaped Notre Dame in its first NCAA game while the Wildcats were running past Pittsburgh, pulled an upset and notched an 80–68 victory. That sent the Spartans to the next round with a 16–8 record, easily the worst of any of the four remaining teams.

For the first time since the week before the ACC Tournament, McGuire had six days to prepare his team for the next game. He would need it—travel arrangements had to be made to the site of the NCAA Championships (no one had yet labeled it the "Final Four") in Kansas City.

O

While Carolina was battling its way through a physically demanding Eastern regional, Kansas expected to have an easier journey through the Midwest regional.

"We had three teams in our conference capable of vying for the national championship," Jayhawks assistant coach Jerry Waugh recalls. "So once we won the conference title, I don't think there was any doubt in anyone's mind that we were going to win the national championship."

Why not?

"We had Wilt Chamberlain."

Kansas also had the advantage of needing only two victories to make it to the national semifinals, compared to North Carolina's three. The NCAA Tournament included 23 teams in 1957, an odd number that required some creative bracketing to make it successful. Teams were bracketed exclusively by region. The East was home to a larger number of highly rated teams, so there were more squads in its bracket (seven) than in the West's (five) or Midwest's (five).

Kansas's path to the championship began in Dallas, where the players discovered that the racial prejudice they had witnessed in Lawrence was minor compared to the tension in the rest of the nation. When Jayhawk administrators began communicating with the host site, they were given a requirement in the form of a suggestion: Perhaps they would be more comfortable at the hotel if the team's two African-American players, Chamberlain and Maurice King, stayed in private homes in the Dallas area. The message was clear: The team hotel in Dallas wasn't willing to accommodate a multiracial squad.

Head coach Dick Harp, who would later join Dean Smith's staff at North Carolina, refused to cooperate. "Forget it," he said. "If we can't stay there together, then none of us are staying there."

The team found another hotel outside Dallas. But this trouble was just a preview of what Kansas would experience in its first regional game, scheduled against Southern Methodist on SMU's home court. The all-white Mustangs were riding a 35-game winning streak in their gym and had finished the regular season ranked fourth in the Associated Press poll.

They almost made it 36. SMU took the game to overtime before succumbing 73–65. More than a half century later, it's not the details of the game that linger, but the actions of the crowd.

"The crowd was brutal," Kansas co-captain John Parker, who said he once saw Chamberlain touch the top of the backboard, wrote in

American Heritage magazine. "We were spat upon, pelted with debris, and subjected to the vilest racial epithets imaginable."

After the game the hostile crowd surrounded the Jayhawk bus. Administrators had to arrange for a motorcycle caravan to escort the team back to the hotel.

The regional championship game against Oklahoma City University was only slightly less tense; the fact that Kansas held the lead throughout the game tempered emotions. Police escorted the Jayhawks off the court and to the airport, and they soon were winging their way back to Lawrence.

Their next stop would be significantly friendlier. Many in the Kansas traveling party thought that they had already achieved their toughest step toward a national championship. The national semifinal matchup with San Francisco—which would have significantly fewer racial implications, as USF coach Phil Woolpert was one of the first coaches anywhere to start three or more black players—would have been intimidating in years past, but the two-time defending champion Dons were without Bill Russell and K. C. Jones. A potential national championship showdown with Carolina was assumed to be a fait accompli.

The Tar Heels had the nation's number one ranking, but the Jayhawks enjoyed two huge advantages. By virtue of playing fewer than 40 miles from campus, they would have an extremely friendly home crowd. And, as Waugh points out, they had another asset impossible to counter: They had Wilt Chamberlain.

Chapter 12
Thirty and One

Carolina fans were willing to pack Woollen Gym to watch their Tar Heels. They were willing to travel to Reynolds Coliseum and beg or plead for tickets to the Dixie Classic or ACC Tournament.

But this was 1957, and the world outside Tobacco Road seemed much larger. It is true that commercial air travel had exploded since the introduction of the DC-3, with the number of Americans flying commercially rising from 3 million in 1940 to 55 million in 1956. But many of those travelers were businessmen flying on corporate expense accounts or upper-class families who had planned their trips well in advance. Raleigh-Durham Airport's first terminal had just opened in 1955; it handled approximately 30 flights per day. The average North Carolinian, even if a crazed basketball fan, simply couldn't arrange to fly from Raleigh to Kansas City with only six days notice.

Carolina students had another option: a chartered bus trip marketed almost exclusively to them, at the steep cost of $43.12 per passenger. Because the semifinals were scheduled for a Friday evening, making the journey would mean missing classes, but interested students had a handy excuse: The head of the institution had already provided his blessing.

"I strongly urge all students who are in proper academic standing and who have the desire to make the trip to Kansas City and help to push our Tar Heel basketball team over the top," Chancellor Robert B. House said.

Unfortunately, this encouragement didn't spark the interest of many Carolina fans. The school sold a total of 86 game tickets for the two-day event. (Teams were guaranteed two games; the losers of the two semifinals met in a third-place contest.) None of the parents of Carolina's starting five attended. Even Carolina head cheerleader Jim Bynum didn't make the trip. Instead, Louie Rosenstock, the student Bynum had beaten in a campus-wide election for the position of head cheerleader, asked to borrow his uniform and megaphone. Bynum agreed, and Rosenstock changed into the uniform in the lavatory of a small Piper Cub airplane he had rented to get to the game.

Given the small size of the Chapel Hill contingent, there were few distractions for the Tar Heels in Kansas City. The night before the semifinal against Michigan State, Frank McGuire gathered his team at the hotel and took the unusual step of showing game film of the Spartans. The overall scouting report was minimal—some basic information about the offense Michigan State would run and its best offensive players. But the video clip, which featured MSU's narrow victory over Notre Dame in the NCAA Tournament, had an unintended impact.

"Showing us that film was one of the only mistakes Coach McGuire made," Lennie Rosenbluth says. "Michigan State looked terrible in that game. After we saw that film, we didn't think much about them. We weren't awed at all, and maybe we should have been."

The Tar Heels also weren't awed by the arena. Municipal Auditorium was large—capacity was 9,287—but dark. Seats along the sideline were limited, though an upper level jutted out over the lower level and provided more sideline seating. In some ways the venue resembled Reynolds Coliseum, minus the vast expanse behind the baskets.

One of the largest media contingents in history was in attendance. McGuire, recognizing a public relations opportunity when he saw one, took the entire group out to dinner on the night before the semifinals.

○

Wilt Chamberlain and the Jayhawks were assigned to the first semifinal. The 7-footer was the evening's star attraction, and there were rumors of tickets changing hands for the exorbitant sum of $50 apiece. Kansas's two season defeats had come courtesy of teams that slowed the tempo and limited Jayhawk possessions. The semifinal opponent, however, was a proud program. San Francisco players were accustomed to winning and—perhaps arrogantly—believed that they could run with Kansas. They quickly found out otherwise.

"They tried to play up-tempo with us," assistant coach Jerry Waugh remembers, "and we beat the blood out of them. You couldn't open up the game against Kansas. Everyone knew that wasn't the way to play against us."

The Jayhawks blitzed the two-time champions 80–56 and advanced to what was expected to be a coronation the next evening. The Tar Heels were already in the arena but saw little of the first game.

"We didn't watch much of it because we didn't want to see it," remembers Bob Cunningham. "Wilty was out there doing his thing, and all we could hear was the crowd roaring. We're down in the locker room getting dressed, and we just hear these periodic roars. We know what that means. We didn't have to see it. If you're going to fight Cassius Clay, you don't want to watch him too long, because [then] you know what you're getting into."

Curious about the undefeated North Carolina team they had heard so much about, most spectators stayed to watch the second semifinal. The Kansas team was less interested.

"Kansas has always been a family," Waugh says. "The coaches and trainers and players were very close. We did things together. So we were going to go out to eat; we weren't going to sit around and watch some other team play."

No matter. Just before game time, a DC-3 owned by Burlington Industries touched down in Kansas City. It carried an illustrious group of North Carolina politicos—governor Luther Hodges, lieutenant governor Luther Barnhardt, and state representative Carl Venters among them. A Greensboro entrepreneur named C. D. Chesley was not in the contingent. He didn't have time—he was too busy at home organizing a revolutionary television package. Chesley had noticed the fever surrounding Carolina's undefeated basketball season. Limited television coverage of the win over Canisius had been available, but he envisioned something bigger. He arranged for a five-station network that would broadcast the semifinal game across the state.

Response was overwhelming. Viewing parties sprouted everywhere. In Chapel Hill, at the Rendezvous Room in the student union, an enormous 32-inch television was available for students. Most dorms had a small television set in the first-floor lounge. Students ringed each set, with a handful trying to appear blasé by lingering in the doorway, chatting and feigning only mild interest. By the time the game was over, however, the hallways and doorways were empty. The facade of coolness had vanished, and students—even those who had pretended to be uninterested in this mere athletic contest—crowded within inches of the screen to see every second of the heart-pounding action.

On Franklin Street Spiro Dorton and a host of students packed into the Goody Shop to cheer on the Tar Heels. The picture was not especially sharp, but the fans didn't care—they were able to watch their team, live, as the game was being played in Kansas City. This truly was the miracle of television.

The only dissenting voice came from the student paper, where the editorial board fancied itself as the lone voice of intellectualism. In a page two staff editorial that ran the morning of the Michigan State game, the writers moaned about a lack of attendance at recent campus events, including speeches by Robert Frost, Dame Edith Sitwell, and Don Shirley. "Not many had enough energy to give education a try," the writers sniffed, "or even to seek a little entertainment more substantial than getting drunk over a winning ball team."

O

If the Tar Heels thought they would breeze to a championship meeting with Kansas, they found out otherwise on one of the first possessions of the semifinal game. Carolina went to its favorite offensive play: get the ball to Rosenbluth. The All-American was being guarded by Michigan State's "Jumpin'" Johnny Green. Rosenbluth wiggled free and prepared to fire a shot and score his first points. Suddenly, Green was soaring through the air. He swatted the shot away—2 points denied and a message sent.

"I had figured this Green kid was just another guy who could jump high," Cunningham says. "But then he jumps and blocks that shot and I remember thinking, 'Whew, they might be a pretty damn good team.'

"They came out all guns firing and sent us a wake-up call real fast. I think they felt like they had nothing to lose, and they played so aggressively."

The Spartans played like a typically physical Big Ten team, but their roster wasn't populated with the type of Midwestern bruisers Carolina fans might have expected. Instead, they had several players with surprising athleticism. Green, in particular, played one of the best defensive games of his career and harassed Rosenbluth all over the floor.

The game was tied 29–29 at halftime. The teams traded the lead throughout the second half and were knotted at 58 as regulation ticked to a close. Michigan State coach Forrest "Forddy" Anderson had made a conscious choice to try to limit Rosenbluth's and Pete Brennan's offensive opportunities. The Spartan game plan was simple: make anyone other than the talented duo beat them. That left Cunningham open for virtually the entire game, which appeared to be a justifiable risk—he had scored more than 10 points just seven times in the previous 30 games.

That stat would not hold. Although Rosenbluth complained about the dim lighting in Kansas City, Cunningham found the shooting environment very attractive. Left to roam the perimeter unguarded, he responded by dropping in a variety of jumpers and layups on his way to a season-high 19 points. He also had another stellar defensive performance, holding Green to only 11 points.

Michigan State forward Jack Quiggle, a fellow All-American, had been MSU's most effective scorer throughout the game and was on his way to a team-high 20 points. With just seconds remaining the Spartans found Quiggle in the backcourt. There was no time to advance into the frontcourt, no time to find a better shot. As the overhead scoreboard ticked from :01 to :00, Quiggle lined up a final shot. He released it, nothing more than a desperation heave destined to soon be forgotten.

Thousands of eyes followed the ball as it flew through the air. Tar Heel players realized that the ball was on-line, that their end-of-game good fortune might have finally expired.

And then it did.

The ball ripped through the net, apparently giving Michigan State a 60–58 win. The Spartans, losers of eight games during the regular season, had toppled undefeated North Carolina.

"The picture wasn't very clear," recalls Buzz Merritt, who watched the game at the Goody Shop. "This was before the days when they would put the clock and the score on the screen, so all we saw was a tie score. Quiggle takes this shot, it goes in, and we think that's it. It looked like the season was over."

A long, impassioned groan filled the room. The heroes were vanquished.

Or were they?

Without the benefit of slow-motion instant replay, officials had only their vision to rely upon. While Michigan State players raised their arms and celebrated and Tar Heel heads hung, the officials conferred. Their judgment was concise: no basket. The referees ruled that Quiggle had released the ball after the buzzer, rendering the shot meaningless. The two teams would have to play five minutes of overtime to determine a winner.

Or maybe more. Both squads scored 6 points in the first extra period, neither able to gain an edge. Although Rosenbluth would finish with 31 points, he struggled to maintain his usual offensive efficiency against the wiry Green.

With both teams tiring, the second overtime was excruciating. Michigan State notched one field goal; Carolina couldn't find the range. With less than 10 seconds remaining, Green went to the line for a one-and-one free throw opportunity. His team held a 66–64 advantage. If he made the first attempt, the game was essentially over. With no three-point shot, one more point would provide an insurmountable margin.

Green toed the line and looked up into the partisan Kansas crowd that had stayed to watch what had turned into a classic. Tommy Kearns stood behind the free throw line, waiting for a potential outlet pass. Just before the ball was handed to Green, one of the Spartan guards approached Kearns. He stood next to the Tar Heel and uttered something softly, so that only the sparkplug guard could hear him: "Thirty and one."

Kearns did not reply. There wasn't much he could say. His team had reeled off 30 straight victories but was now facing defeat a thousand miles from home. One of Michigan State's best free throw shooters was at the line, and even if he happened to miss, Carolina had to go the length of the court and still figure out a way to score in less than 10 seconds.

The odds were improbable.

Players from both sides lined the narrow lane. Brennan secured an inside position. He had been largely overshadowed by Rosenbluth for much of the season but had nonetheless quietly contributed to Carolina basketball history. Brennan, who was matinee-idol handsome, had a personal goal for every game: outrebound his man. He had become the school's all-time leading rebounder earlier in the season; with a championship he would be poised to be a player of national importance during his upcoming senior year.

Green eyed the basket and hoisted the ball. Much like Quiggle's shot at the end of regulation, it looked good. His form was perfect. But the ball bounced off the rim. Brennan hauled down the rebound.

"I knew I had to get down the court fast," he remembers. "So as soon as I got [the ball], I turned and looked up the court. Normally I would've passed it to one of the guards, but I didn't think we had enough time."

The Spartans had expected their star to make the free throw, but they had two guards in the backcourt in case they needed to stop a late Carolina charge. Kearns and Cunningham were ahead of Brennan, but he didn't see them. All he saw was the basket some 75 feet away. He made his way toward it and took a shot from the right of the foul line.

"If we had been in a practice right then, Frank would have called timeout and chewed Pete's ass out about taking a dumb shot," Cunningham says now. "He would've told him to look for the men out in front of him and get the ball up the floor. But thank God Pete didn't follow that strategy. He probably should've gone deeper and tried to throw a bounce pass for a layup. But he pulls up and takes this jumper."

Not just any jumper. A season-preserving jumper. With only three seconds on the clock, the ball dropped through the rim. Spartan shoulders sagged.

In the stands the few Carolina fans in attendance experienced a full range of emotions within a few seconds. Jim Exum, who had seen almost every game that season and had made the 24-hour drive all the way from Chapel Hill, thought his team had finally run out of magic at the 10-second mark.

"Here I am, I'm sitting at the semifinal game," he says. "It looks like we're beat. We're down 2 points, and they have Johnny Green at the foul line. I've driven a whole day to get there, and we're going to lose the first game. I get so disgusted that I get out of my seat and walk out.

I'm walking out of the building, and I hear this tumultuous roar go up. I run back in, and Pete had run down the floor and hit the jump shot to tie it up. I never even saw the shot. I was leaving to go home. I drove 24 hours to get there, and I left before this very memorable shot."

That play finally snapped the will of Michigan State. Carolina took advantage of a very surprising asset—Rosenbluth's defense—in the third overtime. The high-scoring forward made two key steals and turned the steals into two layups. Kearns added a pair of late free throws that gave the Tar Heels a 74–68 lead with 1:32 remaining. Although the Spartans closed the deficit to 74–70 with just under a minute left and Quigg, Cunningham, and Brennan all fouled out, forcing McGuire to go to his bench, Michigan State could get no closer. After 55 minutes of basketball, an exhausted North Carolina had prevailed.

In Chapel Hill an estimated crowd of 2,000 assembled on Franklin Street 15 minutes after the victory. While police officers looked on, fans climbed a stoplight. Toilet paper flew and traffic stopped. Some students had classes to attend in just a few hours (a Tuesday-Thursday-Saturday schedule was common then). Recognizing a golden opportunity when they saw one, they led a march of more than 500 people to the home of chancellor Robert House. Still in good spirits (and with some still holding rolls of toilet paper), the crowd stood outside and shouted, "No Saturday classes!"

House, who had been watching the game, emerged with a smile. "If I didn't think it would do you harm, I'd do it." Classes were held as normal the next day. Attendance was low.

In Kansas City there was nothing more for the Tar Heels to do but shake hands with the Spartans, gather those dark blue travel bags, and walk back to the team hotel. It was after midnight, and the championship game would be played in less than 20 hours.

Some people were already calling the triple-overtime semifinal thriller one of the greatest games in NCAA Tournament history. Yet there were no raucous welcoming celebrations at the hotel. Not a single player from the starting five called his parents; it was simply too late at home to risk bothering them. All that was left was what Rosenbluth had uttered as the team prepared to leave the Municipal Auditorium locker room.

"One more, Coach."

Chapter 13

"The Dream College Game of Our Time"

Tommy Kearns was embarrassed by his performance against Michigan State. He had made only one field goal, committed four personal fouls, and scored only 6 points. During a timeout late in the game, Frank McGuire had looked at his point guard and made an impassioned plea.

"Give me something, Tommy," the coach said. "Please, I need something."

Perhaps fatigued—Kearns played all 55 minutes of the semifinal—the usually feisty guard could not respond.

"I just didn't have enough gas left in the tank," he recalls. "It was just awful."

Kearns slept fitfully on Friday night. Saturday stretched before him; with a 9:00 p.m. Central tip-off, the team would have to kill several hours before departing for the gym. He wandered into the lobby and encountered Jerry Tax, a college basketball writer at *Sports Illustrated*. It was not an especially prestigious assignment at the time, and the winner of that evening's game would not even appear on the cover of the magazine. But Tax's passion for the sport was ahead of its time, and he would stay in his position until 1981, playing a key part in the expansion of *SI*'s college basketball coverage.

Today, writers and players are usually shielded from each other by a phalanx of sports information workers. Interviews are arranged days in advance and tightly controlled. Players are instructed to turn down any requests from the media that are not made through the proper channels. But on the morning of March 23, 1957, there was no need for Jerry Tax to follow any of those formalities. He simply walked down to the lobby of the Continental Hotel, found a comfortable seat, and waited to bump into some players.

One of the first Tar Heels he spotted was Kearns. Many of Kearns's teammates were still asleep. McGuire knew that his team, coming off a triple-overtime game that had lasted well into the night, needed rest before taking on Wilt Chamberlain and the Jayhawks. But Kearns, ever the sparkplug, couldn't be still.

He and Tax traded pleasantries, and then Kearns said something that Tax would never forget: "I know we're underdogs, Jerry" (he was right—Kansas was almost a 10-point favorite). "But we've come too far. We've won too many games that we should have lost. We beat South Carolina early on, we beat Maryland, we beat Duke at home. Even last night, I had a horrible game and we still won. It can't end with a loss. It just can't. It's not going to happen. We're going to win the game tonight."

That statement officially made Kearns one of a handful of people in all of Kansas City who didn't expect Saturday night to be the first major achievement of Chamberlain's career.

"I just had that feeling," Kearns remembers. "We felt like it was going to be our five against their one, and I liked those odds."

While Kearns was predicting victory in the lobby, there was an awkward scene in one of the Continental's suites. A young Kansas alum named Dean Smith, who had played on the Jayhawks' 1952 national championship team, had decided to get into coaching. He got his start by coaching the Kansas freshman team, and after a short tour of duty in the military, he found a job assisting Bob Spear at the Air Force Academy.

Spear was one of those lifer coaches who knew almost everyone in the game of basketball. He encouraged his protégé to develop a similar network, so the pair attended the 1957 NCAA finals together. The final weekend of the college basketball season always coincided with the national coaches convention, so it was much more than just a chance to see two games. For young coaches it was a chance to meet new friends in the business, establish new relationships, and lay the groundwork for future coaching opportunities.

Spear had a set routine for the championship weekend: He roomed with the Naval Academy's Ben Carnevale, University of Denver coach Hoyt Brawner, and Frank McGuire. The foursome had deep ties dating back to their stints in the Navy and would constantly talk basketball in their enormous two-bedroom suite at the Continental. As the tagalong, Smith was required to sleep on a rollaway bed in the living room. For three nights the present and future of Carolina basketball shared a room.

At the time, coaching at the University of North Carolina was not even a remote possibility for Smith. He was just trying to shake enough hands and learn enough names to get a small gateway into the coaching profession. Every opportunity to listen to McGuire talk basketball was important. Making a positive impression was critical.

So far, the most pointed comment McGuire had made to him was, "Who ever heard of anyone named Dean? Where I come from, you become a dean. You're not *named* Dean."

On the day of the game, McGuire asked Smith which team he planned to cheer for that evening. McGuire knew that Smith was a Kansas alum, but he also was aware that Smith's only place to sleep was in the suite living room. It was a question that required delicacy and a precise amount of political savvy—two things for which Smith would not become well known. He was plainspoken and had an unerring way of always doing the right thing, even when it wasn't politically correct.

"I'm going to stay with my alma mater," Smith told McGuire.

The Tar Heels were underdogs even in their own head coach's hotel room.

Regardless, McGuire wasn't concerned about the crowd. He was concerned about Chamberlain. At a team meeting McGuire outlined a defensive strategy that placed Joe Quigg in front of Chamberlain and at least one player behind the 7-footer at all times. The rugged coach had spent many long evenings drilling his team at Woollen Gym on the importance of boxing out for rebounding position, but now he was telling them to forget about those drills.

"When the shot goes up, I want two of you in front of Chamberlain and two of you behind him," McGuire said. "The man farthest away from Chamberlain is to try and chase the rebound."

It was the height of disrespect for the other Jayhawks—Carolina firmly believed that only Chamberlain could beat them.

"We're not playing Kansas tonight," McGuire said. "We're playing Chamberlain. Kansas can't beat you, but Chamberlain can."

Buck Freeman, as usual, knew exactly which tactics his team needed to use to defeat the taller opponent. He pulled Kearns aside.

"Tommy, when you go in against Wilt, take it in at an angle," he told his point guard. "You have a better chance of hitting a bank shot than you do of taking it straight at him."

The Tar Heels wanted not only to contain Chamberlain, but to take him out of his game. Freeman thought back to a game he had seen at the Brooklyn YMCA when a head coach sent his shortest player out to jump center against the opponent's tallest player. It created almost a carnival effect and appeared to rattle the taller player. He mentioned the strategy to McGuire.

At the pregame meal McGuire stared across the table at Kearns, his shortest starter.

"Tommy, are you afraid of Chamberlain?" he asked.

He received exactly the reply he expected: "No, sir."

McGuire barely waited for the words to leave Kearns's mouth.

"Then you're jumping center against him."

O

Kansas took the floor first for pregame warm-ups. The Jayhawks were going through their usual routine when Carolina manager Joel Fleishman walked onto the Municipal Auditorium floor. He surveyed the two benches and began to stack Carolina's equipment on the same bench the team had used the night before. There was only one problem with that arrangement—tournament administrators had already assigned Kansas to that bench, and Fleishman had to move some of the Jayhawks' equipment to make room for Carolina's gear.

Jayhawks head coach Dick Harp spotted the attempted takeover and tried to defuse it.

"That's your bench over there," he said, pointing to the opposite side of the court.

But Fleishman had his orders, and the prospect of staring down Harp was much more appealing than the idea of returning to the Carolina locker room to admit to McGuire that he hadn't secured the correct bench.

"No, sir," the manager replied. "Carolina always uses this bench right here."

Harp was incensed. He located the chairman of the tournament committee, Reeves Peters, who also happened to be the commissioner of the Big Seven Conference. Peters was desperately trying to maintain an air of neutrality despite the arena slowly being filled almost exclusively by Kansas fans. He asked Harp to overlook the perceived slight, take the sportsmanlike approach, and move his team to the opposite bench. Harp complied, but he wasn't happy. McGuire, meanwhile, was nowhere to be found. He was still in the locker room, following his standard practice of not taking the floor until just before the whistle.

"You could see the gamesmanship beginning," Kansas assistant Jerry Waugh recalls. "The whole perception was that they were this Eastern city-slicker team and they were going to come back and take advantage of the Midwestern country bumpkins. They knew how to use that gamesmanship to upset you emotionally and gain an advantage. To us it seemed like a New York mentality of trying to get ahead of somebody without following the rules.

"Dick was already tighter than a two-dollar banjo, and to him this was an upsetting thing. He was feeling the pressure to win the championship because everyone had just assumed it would be handed to him without even trying because of Wilt."

The pressure increased as game time approached. The overflow press corps included an 11-station television network, live radio broadcasts by 73 stations in 11 states, and 64 newspaper writers. One writer estimated that 50,000 tickets could have been sold. It made sense, then, when the public address announcer opened his introductions of the starting lineup by saying, "This is the dream college game of our time."

There was a brief commotion on the Tar Heel bench when North Carolina governor Luther Hodges appeared and took a seat between McGuire and Fleishman. The head coach was miffed at the presence of the governor—who, despite his title, was still an outsider in the world of basketball—but couldn't figure out a way to politely ask him to leave. Hodges stayed on the bench . . . for the moment.

Kansas, wearing the visiting dark uniforms, was introduced first. After being announced each player ran to the free throw line in front of his bench to accept the cheers of the crowd. The Jayhawks received polite applause until Chamberlain was announced. Then a full roar arose from the almost 10,000 fans in attendance. Here was the Goliath they had come to see. He towered almost comically over his teammates, and when the five starters formed a huddle around the free throw line, he was the only player not to lean tightly into the circle.

The Kansas players had run onto the court almost quietly, exchanging businesslike handshakes with each other as they were introduced. Carolina's entrance was less solemn. High fives had not become common practice yet, but there was plenty of back-slapping. The reserves were already beginning to shed their shiny warm-up jackets, even though they knew that they were unlikely to see the floor. Most of the fans in attendance sat quietly as the visitors were introduced. In the stands Dean Smith found a seat next to Bob Spear and Ben Carnevale.

Smith had just gotten comfortable when a ripple went through the crowd. The two teams had taken the floor for the opening tip, and something seemed to be wrong. One of Carolina's shortest players, the little guard wearing the white number 40 jersey, was standing in the center jump circle across from Wilt Chamberlain. Kearns crouched down as if preparing to make a mighty leap. The atmosphere in the arena quickly progressed from confusion to disbelief to amusement.

"When you think about it, it was a really mean thing to do," says Frank Deford, who has written numerous articles on Chamberlain for *Sports Illustrated.* "I know all is fair in love and war, but it probably really hurt Chamberlain. Once again he was being made fun of, and that was something he had to endure everywhere he went. It's not the kind of thing he would have dwelt on for the whole game, but it certainly was the kind of thing that would have been a distraction for him.

"It was mean, but brilliant. Carolina got that initial laugh, and what could Wilt do? He couldn't turn around and say, 'Hey, what are you doing?' If he had done that, he would've taken the bait, and that would have been even worse. So he had to stand there against this guy who is 5-foot-11. All his life Chamberlain had his height pointed out, and now, in this game of games, he's having it really thrown back in his face."

For McGuire it was simple: "I wanted Wilt to wonder if I was crazy," he said.

The Tar Heels dropped the four defenders other than Kearns back to guard the basket. As the referee prepared to throw the ball into the air, Chamberlain stood with his hands on his hips, his back slightly slumped. His posture made him appear closer to 6-foot-8 than 7 feet. He still towered over Kearns.

Chamberlain won the tip, of course. Kearns feinted as if to jump but then dashed back to set up on defense. The giant Jayhawk tipped the ball to a teammate, and the long-awaited showdown between the nation's number one and number two teams was underway.

McGuire knew what had happened to the San Francisco players when they tried to run with Kansas the night before. He preferred an up-tempo style of basketball, but he also preferred to win. His pre-game instructions to his team had been simple: "You don't have to take a shot in the entire first half. We will only shoot the ball if you are in position facing the basket and Chamberlain has been drawn out from under the goal."

Sometimes coaches ask their players to forget about intimidating shot-blockers, to play as if the quality defender isn't there. McGuire did the opposite. No Tar Heel was to attempt a shot unless Chamberlain was in his line of vision. His powerful blocks were a momentum-swinging force in most games; McGuire didn't want to allow the Jayhawks to get on a run and take advantage of the partisan crowd.

Defensively, the plan was simple: make anyone other than Chamberlain beat the Tar Heels. McGuire wanted his team to pack into a tight zone and allow the Jayhawk guards to shoot with impunity. If the Kansas perimeter players got hot, McGuire would adjust on the fly; otherwise, he planned to give them open looks throughout the entire game.

The first Jayhawk possession proved the wisdom of the coach's overall strategy. With Bob Cunningham and Kearns playing at the top of the two-three zone but still so low that they were almost even with the free throw line, open jumpers were available. Rather than attempting a 17-footer, the Jayhawks tossed the ball inside to Chamberlain, where he had set up on the low block in front of Quigg. But as soon as Chamberlain received the ball, Pete Brennan and Lennie Rosenbluth collapsed around him. Chamberlain forced an off-balance shot; it missed badly.

The ensuing possession gave the Tar Heels their first look at Kansas's defensive strategy. Much like McGuire, Jayhawks coach Dick Harp had decided that his squad was essentially facing a one-man team. Looking at the raw numbers, it was a reasonable conclusion. Rosenbluth had led Carolina in scoring in 26 of 31 games prior to the championship. He was the captain, the eventual Helms Foundation Player of the Year, and a member of every All-America team. It was logical that he would be the defensive focus.

"To be a pretty good defensive team was a pride of ours," Waugh remembers. "We wanted to cover Lennie legitimately, but we also knew he was probably the key. Our mentality at Kansas was very defensive. Carolina wanted to take that away from us."

By focusing on the raw numbers, however, the Kansas coaches had failed to notice late-game heroics from some of the other Tar Heels. Brennan averaged a double-double for the season and had made the season-saving shot the evening before against Michigan State, a game in which Cunningham added 19 points. Kearns had made several crucial late-game baskets. Quigg was a reliable force in the post and a consistent double-figure scorer.

Kansas went with what had become a common strategy against the Tar Heels: a box-and-one, with four Jayhawks playing zone and Maurice King, the team's best defender, playing Rosenbluth man-to-man. It took Carolina only a few seconds to diagnose the trick defense. As Cunningham and Kearns passed the ball back and forth at the top of the key, King chased Rosenbluth all over the floor. The Tar Heels made seven passes, and their leading scorer never touched the ball. With the four Jayhawks playing zone packed tightly around the lane, the corners were open—and that's where Kearns found Brennan, who was fouled while attempting a jumper. He dropped through a pair of free throws to give the underdog—yet top-ranked—Tar Heels a 2–0 lead.

As Kansas ran back down the court, it became clear why Chamberlain—who had been a track star at Overbrook High School—was such an offensive force. Even though he inbounded the ball from under the Carolina basket, his long strides quickly carried him downcourt in time to try to establish position between the wary Tar Heel defenders.

Again they collapsed around Chamberlain. Again the other Kansas players appeared reluctant to shoot. Finally, with three Tar Heels surrounding the primary offensive option, King lifted an 18-foot jumper. As he released it Quigg and Rosenbluth made a conscious effort to look for Chamberlain. They shielded him from the rebound as the ball bounced off the rim, allowing Brennan to swoop in and pick up his first rebound of the game.

Brennan had opened the game by demonstrating a willingness to take the corner jump shot that Kansas allowed. But the Jayhawks weren't concerned about that play yet and still wanted anyone other than Rosenbluth to bear the offensive burden. Their four-man zone was slightly more extended than Carolina's arrangement, but not by much. This time it took just four passes—the last a crisp bounce pass from Brennan—for Carolina to find an open man in the corner. With Chamberlain reluctant to leave his position just in front of the basket, Quigg swished a 12-footer from the baseline to give Carolina an early 4–0 lead.

The crowd murmured. This was not in the script. On the Carolina bench the unflappable McGuire was pleased. Other than the fact that the governor of the state of North Carolina was taking up a valuable spot on his bench, the first two minutes of the national championship game had gone very well.

After a scrum for a loose ball, the Jayhawks converted two free throws, but they remained without a field goal. With their primary offensive option taken away, they were having trouble locating good shots.

"I was standing on the foul line, and Tommy was right beside me," Cunningham remembers. "We were challenging their guards to take shots. We were sagging back so far on Wilt, but they kept looking for him. All they had to do was take a few shots and we would've had to go out and play them.

"It was the difference between city ball and other kinds of basketball. If you're from the city, like we were, you know what to do in that situation. You take a few jumpers, you hit them, and the game is over because we've got to come out and guard you, and then you just throw it in to Wilt. But they never adapted to our sagging defense. They couldn't figure out what to do when we took Wilt away from them."

The Kansas defense, meanwhile, was slowly creeping out of its tight formation. King was bouncing around Rosenbluth, effectively taking him out of the offense. The other four Tar Heels were standing around the perimeter of the defense. Other than Rosenbluth, there was very little cutting. Carolina basically wanted to toss the ball around until a Kansas defender failed to rotate. The Tar Heels would be content, it seemed, to take jump shots.

Early in the game, it looked like a sound strategy. Rosenbluth took advantage of the Jayhawks' attentiveness to him and backed King and another teammate down into the lane. That left Quigg open again, this time from a 45-degree angle 10 feet from the basket, and the junior center nailed another uncontested jump shot. The score was 6–2.

"I felt like they were playing into our hands," Cunningham says. "Our strategy on offense was simple: stay away from the middle and stay away from Wilt, because if you challenge him, he will knock it down your throat. Take the ball to the sides and hit those corner shots. When we started hitting those shots, Kansas knew they were getting a game."

The first three minutes gave Dick Harp an uneasy feeling. If Rosenbluth and Chamberlain both had strong performances—as most everyone assumed they would—and cancelled each other out, the game would come down to the lesser-known players on both squads.

So far, Carolina's nonsuperstars were outplaying Kansas's nonsuperstars. The Tar Heels were also trying to control the tempo, so Harp gestured to his guards to move the ball up the court quickly. More possessions meant more touches for Chamberlain. More touches for Chamberlain meant more points. It was a simple formula.

The Jayhawks advanced the ball into the frontcourt quickly. The first option was to look inside to their center. Kansas moved the ball to the wing and created the perfect 45-degree passing angle to feed the post. Chamberlain posted up with Quigg on his hip. But by the time anyone spotted Chamberlain, Kearns and Rosenbluth had blanketed him from the front side and no pass was available. The Jayhawks fired up an ill-advised 18-footer that missed, and Carolina controlled the ball again.

Kansas had pushed the ball up at a near-run; the Tar Heel guards were less hurried. Cunningham half-jogged over midcourt, but as soon as he crossed the center line, he began a slow walk with the ball. The contrast was striking. When Carolina had the ball, everything moved more slowly. The Kansas defenders seemed to be stuck in quicksand.

A Carolina turnover handed the ball back to Kansas. Chamberlain tried a new tactic—rather than post up, where he had learned a trio of defenders awaited him, he flashed to the middle of the lane, looking for a soft spot between the front line and back line of Carolina's two-three defense. The move worked. He received the ball about 8 feet from the basket and had one of his first good looks. But instead of going straight up, he shot a fallaway jumper, and the ball bounced off the rim. With the big man out from under the hoop, Brennan easily gathered the rebound. A Kearns free throw and yet another jumper from the corner gave the Tar Heels a 9–2 lead.

"The way we opened up that game and went ahead so early really shook them," Quigg recalls. "Wilt was playing down, and I was able to hit a couple of jump shots on them. They wanted to play that box-and-one on Lennie, but we were making it tough for them.

"I really felt good. Some games you have that feeling and some games you don't. This was one of those games that I had the feeling. I really felt confident, and all night I felt my touch was there."

Carolina's seemingly passive defense was still frustrating the Jayhawks. After a Kansas timeout Rosenbluth deflected a pass out of bounds, giving Kansas a throw-in on the baseline. The Jayhawks went to one of their standard inbounds plays: Chamberlain stood 3 feet from the basket, waited for the inbounds passer to feed a teammate in the corner, and raised his arms to catch a basic entry pass. Then he turned and easily dropped in a 4-footer over Quigg. Finally, Harp thought, something had worked. The crowd roared. With 4 minutes and 46 seconds elapsed, Chamberlain had his first basket.

For the Tar Heels the play was discouraging in its simplicity. Finally, they had seen an example of what so many other Jayhawk opponents already knew: If Kansas was allowed to execute its offense, and if Chamberlain caught the ball that close to the hoop, there was no way to successfully defend the play.

Kansas remained in the box-and-one defense, which was effectively shutting down Rosenbluth. Harp thought it unlikely that the other Tar Heels would continue their hot shooting. Just then, Kearns made the Jayhawks pay for their sagging defense. As Kearns held the ball 22 feet from the basket, there were no defenders within 4 feet of him. They assumed that there was no need to draw closer. After all, the Tar Heel point guard would just swing the ball lazily around the perimeter; he wasn't a shooter.

Except that he was. Without hesitation, he fired a two-handed push shot toward the rim, his left foot barely leaving the ground and his right foot kicking behind him. The ball swished through the net. The score was 11–4.

Perhaps emboldened, King took a very similar shot. His 20-footer from the left wing also ripped through the net to bring his team back within 5 points.

On the Carolina bench McGuire was both pleased and frustrated. Chamberlain had not touched the ball on two of Kansas's most recent three possessions. The defense that McGuire and Freeman had designed to limit the big man was working as well as they could have hoped. That was the good news. The bad news was that McGuire still had the governor of North Carolina sitting on his right elbow. Hodges seemed like a nice man, but he was making the head coach uncomfortable. McGuire felt the need to temper his sometimes colorful outbursts, and he couldn't coach that way.

His Kansas counterpart did not have similar political problems, but Harp did have a strategic problem. With a third of the first half already gone, the pesky Tar Heels were picking apart his box-and-one defense. He signaled a switch to his team: drop into a more typical two-three zone. The new defense left Chamberlain under the basket, where he discouraged anyone from posting up, but gave the Jayhawks greater flexibility to cover Carolina's hot perimeter shooters.

Of course, this decision also left Rosenbluth to run free. Recognizing the new defense, the Tar Heels swung a couple of passes around the perimeter and then ran a simple zone set. Rosenbluth stationed himself at the top of the key, 20 feet from the hoop. King slowly approached him, expecting more of the lazy ball movement. But then the Carolina star caught a pass from Kearns. Chamberlain crept up almost to the foul line, trying to dissuade Rosenbluth from penetrating.

Rosenbluth didn't want to penetrate. He ripped the ball through, took one hard dribble to his right, and lofted a 17-footer over King, who had not expected the sudden move and was a half step behind. The play was perfect—fast enough to create some space from King, but not deep enough to risk running into Chamberlain. The shot was also perfect, dropping through for Rosenbluth's first points of the game.

Now almost 10 minutes into the half, Kansas was growing more comfortable against the Carolina defense. Chamberlain posted once again on the left block, received a pass, and tried to turn to score. He was fouled and went to the free throw line, where Carolina hoped to make him earn his points. During his professional career Chamberlain would make barely half of his attempts from the line and eventually would turn to a curious underhanded free throw style.

As a collegian, though, he was solid from the stripe for a big man (he converted 62.7 percent of his free throws as a sophomore), and his form looked reasonable. He began with his right foot toeing the line and his left foot split, with the toes of his left foot almost even with the heel of his right foot. He bent his knees, brought the ball almost in front of his forehead, and pushed it toward the basket. On his first trip to the line in the championship game—there would be plenty more, as he finished 11 of 16 from the stripe, double the attempts of anyone else in the game—he converted one of two shots.

With Rosenbluth having drained his first jumper, Harp altered his defense again. He went back to the box-and-one, sending King to harass Rosenbluth. The move took Rosenbluth out of the possession, as he never touched the ball. But by that point the Carolina shooters were swimming in confidence. Kearns and Cunningham tossed the ball back and forth beyond the top of the key, a straightforward two-man game in which the ball never went more than 22 feet from the basket. Kearns caught the final pass in almost the exact spot where he had swished his earlier jumper.

Kansas was no longer content to let the Tar Heels pass the ball with impunity. Kearns soon had a Kansas defender jumping out at him to prevent a repeat performance. The Carolina guard offered a pump fake to lose his defender, took a dribble to his right, and pulled up for another 20-footer that swished through the net.

The Tar Heel lead was 15–7, Carolina's biggest margin of the night. The crowd murmured.

"They got off to such a quick start," Waugh says now. "They were hitting everything they threw up there. They ran out to that 8-point lead, and at that time that was a big lead. Today you just hit a couple of three-pointers and you're right back in it, but we couldn't do that. Eight points seemed like a lot to make up."

It also seemed daunting to young Kansas partisan Dean Smith. Spear and Carnevale were two of the few fans rooting hard for the Tar Heels; these close friends of McGuire wanted to see him win his first national championship. Their boisterous cheers riled Smith, and the three men jabbed each other about strategy and perceived poor officiating like common spectators throughout the first half.

Smith was unable to make any comments on the next Kansas possession, as Chamberlain picked off an offensive rebound but was fouled before he could stick it back in the basket. Carolina had a shallow bench, but the Tar Heels wanted to make the Jayhawk big man earn as many points as possible from the free throw line rather than easy layups. That line of reasoning seemed appropriate when he clanked his first free throw and Rosenbluth soared for the rebound.

By this point Harp was annoyed by Carolina's success against seemingly everything he tried defensively. He sent his team into its third different defense of the half—this time a straight man-to-man. King was still matched up against Rosenbluth, but now all the other Jayhawks also had individual responsibilities. Harp hoped that the switch would not only keep the Tar Heels off the scoreboard, but also encourage them to attack the basket. He knew that it was a risk—Carolina had run successfully against several teams already—but believed that the chance to speed up the tempo was worth it.

His plan did change the activity level of the Carolina offense. Suddenly all five players were in motion rather than four Tar Heels standing around watching Rosenbluth move. Rosenbluth was still the focal point—he whirled around screens and dashed in and around Chamberlain, who mostly remained anchored in the middle. But Kearns and Cunningham also became more active, usually taking one or two probing dribbles before swinging the ball around. A foul away from the ball sent Rosenbluth to the line, where he made both shots.

By now almost frantic, Kansas tried to speed up the game again. This time, it was King taking the inbounds pass and attempting to dribble the length of the court. He veered to the right as he approached the top of the key, got by Kearns, and then lifted an 8-foot jump shot from the baseline. It missed, and because King had run past even Chamberlain on his way down the floor, there were no Jayhawks under the basket to rebound. Brennan, who was well on the way to his goal of outrebounding his man, pulled down yet another ball and dropped it to Kearns. As Kearns began to dribble up the floor, Rosenbluth and Quigg each held out one hand, palm facing their teammate as a signal to slow down.

That wouldn't be a problem, as Kansas went back to a soft two-three zone again. The game ground to a halt. Most of the Jayhawks stood straight up with their hands on their hips, not bothering to get into a defensive stance. Chamberlain still hunched forward, as if he was about to spring into action and swipe the ball, but his position under the goal was 30 feet from where the Tar Heels lobbed the ball back and forth. At one point, after catching the ball on the wing, Rosenbluth cupped the ball in his right hand and rested it against his hip. He looked like he was back on the playgrounds of the Bronx, waiting for the next game to begin.

After it became clear that the Tar Heels had little intention of attacking, the Jayhawks broke out of their zone and began to chase in a man-to-man. Once again, the speed of the game changed noticeably. The Tar Heels were cutting and weaving, moving the ball rapidly from player to player. Each man took a glance at the basket, gauging potential defensive openings before passing the ball. Gone was Kansas's lackadaisical, hands-on-hips defensive attitude. In its place sprouted a frenetic, ball-hawking pace that applied pressure with each pass.

Quigg tried to pull Chamberlain out from the middle. Quigg rarely posted up and spent most of his time at least 10 feet from the basket. But the Kansas big man, aware of his defensive importance, could not be tempted. He stayed within the confines of the painted lane, spreading his arms and providing a formidable disincentive for the Tar Heels to consider crashing the paint.

Only once did he chase. Respecting Quigg's earlier jump-shooting prowess, Chamberlain followed at a safe distance when the Carolina center walked 20 feet from the basket. The Tar Heels reacted immediately—and successfully. This was the epitome of city ball. Pull the big intimidator away from the basket, and there was only one appropriate play: attack. Brennan circled the top of the key, used a screen, and then cut straight down the middle of the lane. His man couldn't keep pace. Brennan raised his hand to signal for a pass at exactly the moment the ball arrived, and he dropped it through for Carolina's easiest basket of the first half.

Rather than back out of the man-to-man immediately because of one layup, Harp stayed with it. He even instructed his team to pressure more intensely, to occasionally make high-risk, high-reward gambles and swipe at the ball while a Tar Heel dribbled it. The plays looked dicey—a defender swiping at the ball left himself out of position and created an opening for his man to drive into the paint. But Harp believed that the risk was actually minimal because no Carolina guard would be willing to penetrate and challenge Chamberlain in the lane.

For the next two minutes, he was right. The Tar Heels were called for an illegal screen while trying to create space on offense, and Kansas nailed four straight free throws to close its deficit to 19–17 with just seven minutes remaining. But Carolina broke its minidrought with a spectacular drive by Brennan, who took advantage of the overplaying defense by taking the ball past two Jayhawks—one of whom was Chamberlain—and penetrating into the lane, where he tossed in a half hook.

The rest of the half followed the same pattern. Carolina would walk the ball up the court and then swing it around the perimeter. No shots were taken without reversing the ball to the opposite side of the floor at least once. Rosenbluth, finally free to operate against the man-to-man defense, made a pair of his patented turnaround jumpers that were almost impossible to defend; with his back to the basket, he jumped and released in the same motion. He could make the shot from 18 feet and beyond, so defenders were in a quandary. If they tightened up on Rosenbluth to try to prevent the turnaround, he might blow by them (as he had done earlier in the game). If they backed off and gave him a step of room, they risked watching the turnaround drop through yet again.

On offense the Jayhawks would sprint down the floor and take a courtesy look into the paint at Chamberlain. If he wasn't immediately available, his teammates jacked up some ill-advised shots. Neither team was corralling many offensive rebounds. The Tar Heels effectively focused their block-out attention on Chamberlain, limiting his ability to get to the ball. On the other end, however, Chamberlain was sweeping most of the missed Tar Heel shots; Carolina players were in such a hurry to retreat down the floor and get into defensive position that they paid little attention to the offensive boards.

Brennan and Chamberlain exchanged free throws at the two-minute mark, leaving the Tar Heels with a 29–22 advantage. Kansas attempted to hold for the last shot of the half, but defensive pressure from Cunningham created a turnover. Carolina had a fast break and a chance to stretch its lead to the biggest of the game. For one of the few times in the game, a Tar Heel guard ran rather than walked the ball up the court, but the team could not convert. King batted away a last-second shot—although Cunningham argued for a foul call—and McGuire and his underdogs took their 7-point lead to the locker room. They had shot an incredible 64.7 percent from the field in the first half, more than 20 percentage points higher than their season average.

In the stands one fan absentmindedly tapped a roughly 40-foot NCAA banner—reading JAYHAWKS ALL THE WAY—that hung on the facade of the upper deck. Then he grabbed his coat and told his friends that he was going to look for another seat. In that moment Dean Smith had decided that, in order to preserve his coaching relationships, he could no longer sit near Spear and Carnevale. Smith wasn't the only one on the move. Governor Hodges, who was used to the civility of politics and not the frankness of a basketball game, eventually got the message. He vacated his seat on the Carolina bench and secured a spot in the stands.

Back in North Carolina, the entire state exhaled. The campus student union was packed. Several Franklin Street establishments had secured a television for the evening. In the Tempo Room, a mellow jazz spot a couple of doors down from the landmark Rathskellar, there was no jazz, just a small television set and a horde of Tar Heel fans. Other familiar aspects of a weekend on campus also had changed. Although a free movie usually was shown twice on Saturday night, there was but one viewing of *Blackboard Jungle* on March 23, at 7:30 p.m. Students had something better to watch after that.

In Albemarle Woody Durham and his father watched the limited halftime programming. One of the announcers offered what seemed like an absurd opinion: "I wouldn't be surprised to see another triple-overtime game."

Durham's father snorted and looked at his son. "By God," he told Woody, "if that happens, I may not live to see the end of it."

Chapter 14

The Epic
Conclusion

In the cramped Municipal Auditorium locker room, Frank McGuire was pleased.

The most obvious source of the good humor was his team's 7-point lead. With no three-point shot and no shot clock, it was a sizable margin. At minimum, he thought, the Jayhawks would have to play catch-up for most of the second half. He had reliable guards who would take care of the basketball; that should prevent any overwhelming Kansas momentum. His players had largely kept the partisan Kansas City crowd out of the game, and they had done as good a job as possible on Wilt Chamberlain. The Kansas standout had gotten some points, of course, but he also had occasionally looked frustrated. By making Chamberlain earn his points at the foul line, the Tar Heels would probably hold the big man under his 29.6 points per game average.

. Of course, if McGuire wanted to continue sending Chamberlain to the free throw line, fouls would eventually become a problem. The coach had used Danny Lotz briefly in the first half, but as usual had gone almost exclusively with his five starters. Rosenbluth had picked up two fouls already; an early second-half foul on him would be crippling.

The game resumed with another jump ball. Chamberlain walked to the center circle looking almost wary. Tommy Kearns also walked toward center court . . . but then he dropped back and took up a defensive position in front of the Kansas basket. Sending the little man out to jump center had been funny—and maybe even productive—the first time. Now just 20 minutes remained to determine a national champion. McGuire decided to play it safe, keep Kearns back for defense, and concede the tip. Chamberlain, this time standing to his full height, easily outjumped Joe Quigg to begin the half.

The Jayhawks began it exactly the way they had planned: by dumping the ball inside to their star. Chamberlain was instantly double-teamed. Kearns swiped at the ball and was whistled for a foul, but Chamberlain failed to convert his free throws, and Lennie Rosenbluth skied for the rebound.

Kansas went back to the man-to-man defense, which had been somewhat effective in the first half. They could no longer afford to sit back and dare Carolina's shooters to beat them. For one of the few times all night, the Tar Heels tossed the ball to Quigg in the paint. He turned to face Chamberlain and succeeded in getting the ball past the intimidating shot-blocker, but Quigg still had to alter his shot. The ball bounded off the rim.

It quickly became obvious why McGuire had been so intent on controlling the tempo. After rebounding the missed shot, the Jayhawks rushed into the frontcourt and converted a pullup jumper before the Carolina five had all crossed midcourt. The next Tar Heel possession ended in another failure to score, as Rosenbluth tried a sweeping hook shot. It was a shot he had made regularly during the season, but on this occasion he had to loft it high enough to get it over the outstretched arm of Chamberlain. The extra height caused the ball to bounce off the rim.

Chamberlain grabbed the rebound, his second of the half. He was beginning to control the game. After throwing an outlet pass to start the fast break, he glided down the court. Kansas moved the ball to the corner and waited for him to split the lane. As soon as he moved into scoring position, he raised his hand to signal for the ball. The pass arrived high. Both Chamberlain and Brennan jumped to catch the ball, but only Chamberlain had a real chance at it. He caught it, landed, and then jumped again to drop the ball into the hoop and close the Carolina lead to 29–26.

Today, we might call this play the forerunner of the alley-oop, a tactic that Kansas assistant Jerry Waugh regrets the Jayhawks didn't have in their arsenal back then. "It just wasn't something you did in the game of basketball at that time," he says. "If we had done it, there's no question it would have worked. Just throw the ball up, let him go get it, and put it in. No one could have jumped with Wilt in 1957."

Chamberlain, by now brimming with confidence, was turning into the player who had terrorized the Big Seven Conference for most of the season. Brennan, who was frantically calling for the ball, got too aggressive on Carolina's next possession and drove into the lane. The big man was waiting and viciously swatted Brennan's shot out of bounds.

Quigg made a baseline jumper to restore the 5-point lead, but it was clear that the momentum was changing. Kansas's man-to-man defense was denying some of the open shots Carolina had utilized earlier in the game. Missed Tar Heel shots were leading to Jayhawk fast breaks, and those fast breaks were producing much better scoring opportunities for Chamberlain, who could operate effectively without three defenders draped on him. Carolina players also were starting to lose their composure in front of the hostile Kansas City crowd. When Quigg was whistled for a foul on the next Kansas possession, he whirled around with his head in his hands to protest the call. Across the lane Cunningham slapped both hands on his knees and then threw his hands in the air to signify his own displeasure with the ruling.

A Tar Heel turnover and a pair of Chamberlain free throws after a Quigg foul (which prompted McGuire to turn to Lotz off the bench in an effort to preserve his junior starter for later in the game) brought the score to 31–30. The Jayhawks were within 1 point of Carolina with 16:43 remaining.

With Lotz standing 35 feet from the basket, Brennan was able to drive the baseline without fear of Chamberlain repeating his earlier rejection. Brennan converted a twisting layup to provide some brief breathing room. Injecting an important burst of energy, Lotz tipped a potential offensive rebound away from Chamberlain under the Kansas basket and then celebrated by pumping his fist in the air.

The Tar Heels initiated a nearly two-minute possession. It wasn't exactly a "freeze," the era's term for a stall, but it was close. Carolina players did look at the basket occasionally, but if there wasn't a substantial opening, they continued to pass the ball around the perimeter. McGuire probably would have called it "control basketball," a term he defined in his book *Offensive Basketball*:

The principle is to spread the defense and allow the man with the ball plenty of room in which to operate. Opponents are kept busy so they will not have time to attempt to double-team the man with the ball. When possible, the man with the ball is given the whole side of the court to himself so that he may use one-on-one tactics to keep the ball or break free for a sure shot.

The process was methodical. Rosenbluth continued cutting back and forth across the lane and eventually pinned King on his hip at the free throw line. As soon as Rosenbluth, who had his back to the basket, received the pass from Cunningham, King's indecision was apparent. First he stepped toward the most dangerous Tar Heel, leery of his turnaround jumper. Then King stepped back, concerned about a drive. In the moment that King was back on his heels, Rosenbluth swung the ball to his right hand, stepped hard to the basket, took two dribbles, and lobbed a one-handed snowbird into the hoop. The scoring gap was back to 5 points, but less than 15 minutes remained on the clock.

Despite the lead Carolina was wilting. Buoyed by suddenly reliable outside shooting, the Jayhawks went on a 10–2 run over the next five minutes. The strategy of making Chamberlain earn his points at the free throw line successfully limited his scoring, but it also rapidly inflated the foul total for several key Tar Heels. Both Kearns and Rosenbluth had three fouls, and Quigg had four. With 10:20 left in the game, Kansas held a 40–37 lead.

"We were in a precarious position," McGuire later said. "We had played a triple overtime the night before in the semifinal against Michigan State. The boys were tired. We also had a bad foul situation.

"As I see it, Kansas should have pressed that foul situation, and also taken advantage of our weariness. They had the momentum, after eating up our 29–22 halftime lead and going in front themselves."

That wasn't how Kansas coach Dick Harp saw it. His team had trailed throughout the first half but had finally taken the lead. Many of Carolina's points had been generated by what he thought was uncharacteristically good outside shooting. With Chamberlain beginning to dominate the paint defensively, Harp believed that a 40–37 lead was sizable. So instead of pressuring the Tar Heels, he took his foot off the

gas pedal. With 7:30 remaining, he moved his team into a straightforward freeze. The Jayhawks had no interest in shooting; they would
simply melt the clock while Carolina looked on helplessly.

"It was a decision made by Coach Harp," Waugh recalls. "He felt
if they were still going to sit back in that zone defense while we had
the lead, he was going to let them play that way and take the win.
Some people might say, 'Why not try to run them?' But we wanted to
bring them out of that zone so we could use Chamberlain."

The Municipal Auditorium crowd loved the strategy. The
championship seemed within reach.

Someone else also loved the Kansas strategy—Frank McGuire.

Wondering how they would defend the freeze, the Carolina
guards looked over at their head coach. He raised his right hand, all
five fingers outstretched. The message was clear: Let them hold the
ball until five minutes remained.

"Kansas made a strategic error," Kearns says. "Instead of coming
after us, [they] let us rest."

The rest was exactly what Carolina needed. For two minutes the
Tar Heels were able to put their hands on their knees and catch a second wind. McGuire would later lob a soft criticism at Harp's tactic in
his second book, *Defensive Basketball:*

Some coaches initiate a stall attack when they are as much as ten
points ahead of a dangerous opponent and when there is as much
time as seven or eight minutes left to play. Many coaches believe
that this is folly and that a team should never change its offense or
pace when it is winning. The wisdom of the change from a successful
attack to a stall offense is certainly debatable, but conditions govern
many such decisions and it is just one more of the game problems
facing the coach.

As McGuire insinuated, Harp's choice would be debated for many
years. It was successful in one sense—Carolina wasn't able to cut into

the three-point advantage Kansas held. Then, with 1:45 remaining on the clock, a seemingly championship-clinching moment transpired: Lennie Rosenbluth picked up his fifth foul while trying to stop a layup attempt, sending him to the bench for the remainder of the game.

"I picked up some stupid fouls in that game," Rosenbluth remembers. "Normally, I never would have fouled out of a game. That last foul was desperation, but it was a stupid foul."

After being whistled for his fifth infraction, Rosenbluth had to make the long walk from the Kansas basket to the Carolina bench at the other end of the court. But he didn't make it alone. Before he could cross midcourt, Maurice King was walking beside him, shaking his hand and throwing a sympathetic arm around his shoulders. Several other Jayhawks extended a right hand in admiration of Rosenbluth's effort—20 points, second only to Chamberlain's scoring output in the game. By the time Rosenbluth reached the Tar Heel bench, the entire arena was showering him with a standing ovation.

With Kansas captain Gene Elstun on the free throw line, victory was imminent. Chamberlain spotted a friend in the stands and smiled, confident that he was about to win his first college championship. But Elstun missed both free throws, and the Jayhawks would score just 2 more points in regulation. Meanwhile, the Tar Heels chipped in a field goal and a free throw. The Jayhawks expected little from Rosenbluth's replacement, Bob Young; the savvy senior took advantage by driving to the basket for a quick layup. The game was tied at 46 when Carolina began its final possession.

The primary offensive option, Rosenbluth, was on the bench. The ball found Cunningham, who had not yet made a field goal.

"I'll never forget it," he says now. "I took [a shot] from the top of the key on the left side. The ball went down. I swear to God, it went down, went around, and bounced back out. I grabbed the rebound, went back up, and Wilt knocked me about three rows back. The buzzer went off, and they never blew the whistle. Thank God they didn't. I probably would have died if I would have had to go to the foul line."

Overtime—and yet another jump ball—was needed to decide the champion. The Tempo Room in Chapel Hill was silent and tense. In the student union Carolina students paced around the room to work out their stress. Franklin Street bars were in a bind: By city ordinance, drinks could not be served after 11:45 p.m., but no fans were leaving.

Inside Municipal Auditorium Alfred Hamilton, one of the few Carolina fans in attendance, had to step into the concourse to relieve some of his anxiety. Dean Smith desperately wanted to discuss some of the strategy he had seen over the previous 40 minutes with Carnevale and Spear, but he knew that their friendship would be tested by a national championship overtime and wisely stayed in the seat he had found at halftime.

When the third jump ball descended, Chamberlain won the tip, but King missed a leaning jumper. Cunningham grabbed the rebound, giving Carolina its first chance to surge ahead since midway through the second half. It was not to be. The teams exchanged baskets. Carolina then melted nearly a minute off the clock before beginning what could have been the winning possession. Kearns's dribble penetration failed to soften the Kansas defense, however, and Chamberlain blocked a last-second shot attempt. The teams remained knotted at 48 when the buzzer sounded.

Each team had managed just one basket. Despite the second-half slowdown, the intensity of the contest and back-to-back games were beginning to create exhaustion. As the players walked to their benches with shoulders slumped, the public address announcer boomed, "Fans, these teams are putting on a great show. Let's give them a big hand." The crowd roared.

O

Even against Kansas's extended man-to-man defense, the Tar Heels still looked like the quicker team when the second overtime began one minute later. Kearns made the first attempt at penetration, but when Chamberlain took one imposing step forward to the free throw line, the little Carolina point guard circled back to the midcourt stripe. The play ended on a turnover. On the bench, McGuire knew that his team probably could not survive many more empty possessions.

Yet Kansas was looking weary. A long Jayhawk jump shot failed, and Brennan boxed out Chamberlain. The Dipper tried to sky over his shorter defender's back and was whistled for a foul.

He compensated for the mistake on Carolina's next possession. The Tar Heels isolated Quigg on the baseline. The Carolina center turned his back to Chamberlain, then pivoted and tried to beat his man to the basket. As Quigg began to lift off for a hook shot, Chamberlain swooped into his line of vision, one arm held high above his head in prime shot-swatting position. Quigg hesitated for just a moment, and that brief second of hesitation caused him to travel. Another Carolina turnover.

With under three minutes remaining, it looked like one basket could win the game. Harp called a timeout to set his offense and make sure his superstar didn't go the entire five-minute extra period without getting a good shot opportunity. On the Carolina bench, Rosenbluth finally understood the plight of Tar Heel fans who had followed his team through 31 victories.

"That was the first time I felt what the fans were going through," he said. "I had to sit there and watch it, and all I could think was, 'Come on guys, please do it.' That's when I started to feel the tension. But at the same time, I didn't have any hesitation that we were going to win. We fell behind and won all the time. So this wasn't unusual. I knew we would do it; I just wasn't sure exactly how we would do it."

The sagging Carolina two-three defense forced a Chamberlain turnover, as he was surrounded on a shot attempt and made an ill-advised pass that sailed out of bounds. The Tar Heels regained control for what could have been the last time in the game. They passed the ball around the perimeter with their usual patience. With each pass the Carolina bench grew more animated. Coaches and players almost always stayed seated, but finally Rosenbluth couldn't take it—he stood and pointed out a couple of potential defensive weaknesses to his teammates.

With 1:02 remaining in the second overtime, Kearns began to penetrate and drew a foul. With Rosenbluth out and the Jayhawk defense now keying on Brennan, a free throw was perhaps Carolina's best chance to generate quality offense. But Kearns's shot pinged off the back of the rim, and Chamberlain corralled the rebound with two hands.

Kansas's intentions were clear—get the ball to Chamberlain. Five feet from the goal, he secured a pass while facing the Jayhawk bench, with his back to the basket. This was prime Wilt Chamberlain scoring territory. Maybe he would shoot a turnaround, or perhaps a hook shot, or maybe an up-and-under. Cunningham, though, had no intention of waiting to see what might come out of the offensive arsenal. He dashed across the lane and swiped at the ball with both hands.

Cunningham had a dual purpose: First, he thought he might take the big man by surprise and get an easy steal. Failing that, he wanted to commit the foul hard enough to prevent a shot—just as McGuire had taught him in practice—and force Chamberlain to the free throw line. Cunningham arrived just as Brennan, the nearest man to the Kansas center, began whacking at the ball. Their combined efforts made it look like a very physical play.

Chamberlain, who was already frustrated, took exception. He stepped toward Brennan. The feisty New Yorker didn't back down, and suddenly there was a melee under the Kansas basket. Tied at 48 with less than one minute to play, the teams appeared ready to slug it out to determine the national championship.

Louie Rosenstock, the substitute cheerleader, acted on instinct when he saw Brennan in trouble. He bounced up from his position beneath the basket and jammed the small end of his borrowed megaphone into Chamberlain's stomach. In reaction, the Jayhawk's knee hit Rosenstock in the teeth; the scar from this unexpected bite would stay with Chamberlain for the rest of his life.

Harp bolted off his bench when he saw Brennan and Chamberlain being restrained by teammates. Spotting the opposite coach in the fray, McGuire also left his bench and trotted the length of the floor to ascertain the situation. The two men—Harp the caretaker of the Phog Allen legacy, McGuire the man who constantly preached sportsmanship—were soon nose-to-nose.

"I just wanted to prevent a fight," Harp would say later.

Accounts of exactly what happened in front of the Jayhawk bench varied. Kansas representatives claimed that McGuire had used harsh language. McGuire said that someone on the Kansas bench told him to "shut up" and that another person had hit him in the stomach. As flashbulbs popped wildly, tournament chairman Reeves Peters left his seat to try to restore order.

Game officials quickly defused the confrontation, and Brennan offered Chamberlain a handshake—which the big man accepted, engulfing Brennan's hand with his enormous grip—to show that there were no hard feelings. A few moments later, Harp and McGuire also met at the scorer's table to shake hands.

"It was just the tension of the game," McGuire said later that evening.

While Harp was walking back to his bench, Chamberlain was already toeing the free throw line with his right foot to begin his shooting motion. Even before he released the ball, it was obvious that his mechanics were askew. He never shot the ball with much arc, and his free throws rarely made it above the square on the backboard. But this attempt was even flatter than usual, and it clunked off the underside of the rim. That made it a difficult shot to rebound, but Young secured the ball.

McGuire intended to hold the ball for the final shot, but a Carolina turnover gave Kansas yet another chance with less than 10 seconds to play. The Jayhawks called a timeout with six seconds left and inbounded the ball from midcourt. Ron Loneski's shot failed, leaving the game tied at 48. Improbably, Carolina had survived nearly 12 minutes without Rosenbluth. Each team had used just seven players in the second overtime.

O

Again, the teams were allotted only one minute of rest. Chamberlain looked winded as the third five-minute period began, and Quigg nearly outjumped him for the session's first possession. But even a winded 7-footer had an advantage over the 6-foot-9 Quigg, and the Jayhawks garnered the first scoring opportunity. It failed, as King missed a 21-footer.

Harp had instructed his players to increase the defensive pressure, and they pushed their man-to-man defense beyond the midcourt stripe. The strategy had its benefits: If the Jayhawks could create a turnover, they might get an easy layup, and with scoring chances scarce, a layup could be the margin of victory. But the plan was also risky. By stretching the passing lanes, Kansas increased the chances of a Carolina backdoor cut, which also could lead to an easy layup. Whatever happened, it seemed inevitable that the third overtime would be the deciding period.

With Quigg still pulling Chamberlain away from the basket, Kearns took advantage of the extended defense and drove to the hoop. His right-handed layup banked off the glass and through the net, giving Carolina what felt like an enormous 50–48 lead. Rosenbluth bounded off the bench to implore his team to play defense.

The deficit seemed to cause the Jayhawks to tighten. With only a momentary glance at Chamberlain inside, Elstun fired a 17-footer that clanked off the back rim. Quigg rebounded, giving the Tar Heels a tremendous edge: a 2-point lead plus possession of the basketball.

Now bordering on frantic, Kansas contested every Carolina pass. Forty feet from the basket, Kearns curled off a screen to receive a handoff from Quigg. He appeared to gain a step on his man and started to penetrate. Before he could reach the underbelly of the Kansas defense, he was fouled.

Three minutes and 47 seconds remained.

Kearns's first free throw was good. He fired the second shot and began backing up, Rosenbluth-style, before it even reached the rim. He knew it was good—and it was, giving Carolina a 52–48 lead, the biggest advantage either side had enjoyed in almost 15 minutes of game action. Less than four minutes to the championship.

This time, however, there would be no ill-advised Kansas jump shot. The Jayhawks passed up several looks from the perimeter in an effort to feed Chamberlain. Eventually, Loneski dispensed with the notion of a proper entry pass and simply lobbed the ball in Chamberlain's vicinity and allowed him to go get it. With one dribble the gazellelike center was gliding to the hoop, where he laid in a one-handed scoop shot and drew a foul on Young. The Tar Heels had enjoyed their 4-point lead for just 20 seconds. The crowd was on its feet and roaring. Chamberlain's free throw cut the Kansas deficit to 1 point.

Kearns strutted up the court, using a high dribble and bouncing the ball above his waist. Now he was a firefly, darting in and out of the lane with the ball but avoiding potential turnovers. He left the ball for Cunningham, who was not as smooth and narrowly avoided a Kansas steal near midcourt. Seeing his tentativeness, the Jayhawks sent a double-team to trap Cunningham. But instead of creating a turnover, their pressure led to a foul. He went to the free throw line with a chance to give his team a 3-point lead with 2:50 remaining.

Cunningham was the least reliable free throw shooter of the starting five; while the rest boasted percentages above 70, his hovered at 56. Facing a one-and-one, he showed why, as his first attempt missed everything and sailed out of bounds. Kansas had survived and now had an opportunity to retake the lead.

The Jayhawks' plan was not complex: They posted Chamberlain 8 feet from the basket, tossed him the ball, and waited for him to operate. As he spun to face the hoop, he spotted Loneski under the net. Two pairs of arms were swatting at Chamberlain, whereas Loneski seemingly had an open layup. Chamberlain dropped the ball to his teammate. It was the perfect high-low play; even while the pass was on its way to Loneski, the Kansas reserves were springing off the bench, prepared to celebrate.

But Young contested the shot, and Loneski fired it too hard off the backboard. With two Tar Heels blanketing Chamberlain and Young out of position due to the block attempt, there was no weak-side rebounding help. King grabbed one of the few Jayhawk offensive rebounds of the day. Fearing an easy putback, Brennan—who already had been targeted by the crowd for his earlier confrontation with Chamberlain—swatted King before he could score the points.

Two minutes and 33 seconds remained.

King's first free throw was perfect, tying the score at 52. His second, however, was off to the left and too hard. Quigg pulled down the rebound. After 52 minutes and 30 seconds of basketball, the nation's two best teams remained tied.

With no Rosenbluth, Kearns was the offense's best initiator. He pounded the ball, usually with his right hand, 35 feet from the hoop. He was doing his jitterbug routine again, occasionally taking a hard step toward the basket to gauge the responsiveness of the Kansas defense. But by now the Jayhawks were wary of his dribble penetration and gave him a wide berth. Eventually, even Chamberlain came out from his post under the basket to provide some defensive help.

That forced Kearns into a tactical error. He left the ball for Quigg without realizing that the Tar Heel center was pinned against the sideline 38 feet from the goal. Quigg, not used to handling the ball that far from the basket, immediately was met by a Jayhawk double-team that included the spidery Chamberlain. Guard John Parker took advantage of Quigg's indecision and stole the ball cleanly. He found King across the court; King brought the ball across the time line, and Harp stood to call timeout. The Kansas bench was euphoric. Finally, it seemed, they could put the game out of reach. Less than 90 seconds remained, and they had possession. The plan was obvious to everyone, including Carolina: get the ball to Wilt Chamberlain.

It was five minutes past midnight in Chapel Hill.

When play resumed Parker and King passed the ball back and forth at the top of the Carolina defense. The Tar Heels initially refused to chase; they knew that it was merely a setup to establishing better position for Chamberlain.

Eventually, though, Carolina went to a more aggressive version of the zone. Kearns and Cunningham crept above the foul line, even double-teaming Gene Elstun at one point to try to force a turnover. McGuire had decided that he had two options: His team could sit back, watch Kansas hold for the last shot, and hope Chamberlain missed, or they could try to control the game by increasing the defensive pressure. The latter choice was risky because it could lead to an easy layup, but not much riskier than crossing their fingers and hoping Chamberlain missed in the final seconds.

The Tar Heels couldn't coax a turnover, and the stretched defense allowed Chamberlain to receive the ball 8 feet from the basket in the middle of the lane. He turned quickly, elevated, and bumped into Quigg. The ball never reached the rim, but there was no whistle. Carolina had a chance to secure the loose ball as it trickled toward the sideline, but in the scrum no one could get a handle on it. Everyone on the Kansas bench leapt to his feet to assist the officials with the call; perhaps realizing that Quigg's foul had been overlooked, the referees awarded the ball to the Jayhawks.

Kansas ran a set play, and again Carolina pressured. The ball found Elstun on the sideline in front of the Kansas bench. He looked indecisive. Chamberlain was covered—Quigg was behind him and Brennan in front. Elstun took one dribble and shuffled a few feet down the sideline. Kearns rotated over, intending to put tough pressure on Elstun, who had picked up his dribble and had nowhere to go. He looked back to the top of the key for an outlet. Kearns leaped, hoping to intercept a pass. But the fiery Carolina point guard mistimed his jump and came crashing down on top of Elstun.

The play happened directly in front of the Kansas bench, and for a moment it looked like another bench-clearing brawl was imminent. The force of the collision knocked Elstun off the playing floor and into his bench while the Jayhawk reserves stood and screamed at Kearns. Not intimidated, Kearns aided Elstun's fall with a dismissive shove, right arm fully outstretched.

The crowd roared. More than 10,000 fans had paid for a simple basketball game. Instead, they were getting a classic, plus one near riot and now another shoving match. By that point, however, most of the players on the floor were too tired to fight. The situation was quickly defused, and Kearns was whistled for a foul. With 31 seconds left in the third overtime, Elstun went to the free throw line with a chance to give his team a 2-point lead. He was a 65.2 percent free throw shooter.

The crowd fell silent. There was no elaborate free throw routine, just a spin of the ball and the guard's right hand pushing the ball toward the basket. From the moment it left his fingers, its flight was clear—it was too long. Parker, who had lined up several feet behind the free throw shooter, saw immediately that the shot was too hard. He swung his right leg in the air and leaned back as if to will the ball into the basket. But it did not cooperate. The ball bounded off the back of the rim and dropped into the hands of Bob Young, who had taken up the outside free throw position next to Chamberlain.

Elstun had one more shot, its importance magnified by the preceding miss. Same routine, same quiet crowd; the fans had let out an audible gasp after the first shot but now were channeling positive thoughts to the 6-foot-3 forward.

This shot was pure. There was no need for body language. It swished through the net, and Kansas had a 53–52 advantage. The Tar Heels inbounded the ball and called a timeout. Twenty-eight seconds remained.

With Rosenbluth out, one of Carolina's few offensive sets—"feed the monster," as they called setting up their star—was eliminated. McGuire wanted an equally simplistic set. He liked Kearns's quickness against Parker. He told the four other Tar Heels to spread the floor and be ready for a potential kick-out pass from Kearns. But if the scrappy guard saw an alley, just like on the New York playground, McGuire wanted him to go all the way to the basket, directly into Chamberlain's territory, and challenge the big man.

It was an audacious plan. It looked even riskier when Quigg—who was standing directly in front of the Carolina bench, 20 feet from the basket—was unable to draw Chamberlain away from the hoop.

But Kearns didn't want to abort the plan. He had waited too long for the opportunity to take the big shot, having struggled throughout his sophomore season and even thought about transferring. Now he had the situation he loved—the ball in his hands and the potential to win the game. Like McGuire, he believed that he could beat Parker.

Kearns bounced the ball with his right hand 25 feet from the basket. Parker stepped up to apply pressure. Kearns turned with his left shoulder and shifted the ball to his left hand. Suddenly, he was spinning. Parker had overcommitted. With the rest of his teammates watching helplessly, Kearns blew by Parker and into a clear path to the basket. Spreading the floor had worked perfectly.

Except for Chamberlain.

The most intimidating defensive player in basketball had his right foot in the lane and his left arm pointed toward Quigg near the Carolina bench. He was concerned about his man, but he was even more concerned about the whirling point guard who was trying to invade his territory. The 5-foot-11 Tar Heel split the lane just to the left of the basket and steamed toward the 7-foot Jayhawk center.

Chamberlain jumped off both of his feet at the same time that Kearns elevated off his right foot. Kearns's momentum carried him past Chamberlain, and for the briefest of moments it looked like he might be able to loft the ball toward the basket with his left hand. But Chamberlain swatted at the ball with his right arm in an almost dismissive motion. The ball rocketed out of bounds; Chamberlain never even looked at the basket. He finished the play still facing away from the hoop, never glancing at the baseline where Kearns's momentum had carried him out of bounds.

The ball remained with the Tar Heels, but now they had less than 15 seconds to preserve the perfect season.

This time, no timeout. From under the basket the ball was inbounded to Young along the baseline. He took two right-handed dribbles and found Quigg a step left of the free throw line, at what would eventually become known in basketball terminology as the left elbow.

Prior to that night, Quigg had seen Chamberlain play only in news reels. He vividly remembers his reaction the first time he saw the athletic center gliding around the court. Sitting in a darkened Chapel Hill movie theater, Quigg saw the face of college basketball changing. "I started practicing my jump shot," Quigg says. "I knew he would turn me into an outside player."

Chamberlain bit on the play—he was guarding Quigg tightly, and the paint area was wide open. Quigg processed the situation and knew immediately what to do: give Chamberlain a head fake. If he went for it, try to jet around him for a layup at the unprotected goal. The safe play was a jump shot, just as Quigg had seen on the highlight footage. But it wasn't the right play.

Chamberlain went for the fake. He moved toward Quigg with one big step, the same preleap preparation he had made before blocking Kearns's shot. Although it provided him with an extra inch or two on his leap, the step also put Chamberlain off-balance. Quigg waited for him to raise his arms, then took one hard dribble to the right. He had Chamberlain on his left hip and no one else in front of the basket. He took a step with his right foot, then his left, and began to elevate.

Chamberlain came from behind, unwilling to let his man have a free championship-clinching layup. He rejected Quigg's shot with his right hand, and for half a second it appeared to be a clean play. But the official's whistle came next, his right arm shooting up to signal a foul. King had come over to help and banged Quigg with the body, and while Chamberlain might have blocked the ball cleanly with his right arm, his body and left hand had made contact with Quigg. The contact could not be ignored, even in the closing seconds of a title game just minutes from the Kansas campus.

It was a shooting foul—two shots for Carolina's junior center. The overhead scoreboard showed 0:06 remaining.

Quigg was a 72.1% free throw shooter but had attempted only 104 all season—just a third of Rosenbluth's total and less than even Kearns. Quigg's form was not particularly artistic, but he seemed to have a knack for pushing the ball through the hoop. The crowd stood. These would be the two biggest free throws of the basketball season.

Frank McGuire wanted a timeout. In many ways it was curious timing. It seemed more appropriate for the opposing coach to call timeout, perhaps to try to build more pressure on the shooter. There was little strategy that could be imparted; the break served only to allow Quigg 60 extra seconds to think about his shots.

"McGuire was thinking all positive, no negative," Rosenbluth recalls. "He wanted to talk about what we would do when Joe made the shots."

The Carolina coaching staff was made for this type of situation. McGuire was the master psychologist; he knew how to read body language, knew exactly what his players needed and how they would respond to specific circumstances. Freeman, the tactician, was already thinking several moves ahead, his mind processing every possible permutation.

McGuire had assembled a team in his own image, a group of brash New Yorkers with plenty of confidence. But after 54 minutes and 54 seconds of basketball, he wondered if he might encounter self-doubt.

Quigg jogged to the huddle. "I'm going to make them, Coach," he said.

McGuire allowed himself the briefest of smiles. "All right," he said, gathering the team around him. "Now, when Joe makes these two shots, this is what we're going to do. They're going to come down the floor and they're going to look for Wilt. Joe, I want you to get behind Wilt, and Danny, you get in front of him. Once Joe makes these free throws, that's what they're going to do."

The horn sounded, and the Tar Heels broke their huddle. McGuire sent Lotz into the game to replace Young. Just before Quigg walked back onto the floor, Freeman touched his arm. He wanted to emphasize one final point of technique.

"Get up on your toes when you shoot, Joe," he said.

The crowd had buzzed during the timeout but grew mostly silent when the official handed Quigg the ball. Just as Freeman had instructed, he did lift ever so slightly onto his toes when he took the first shot. It made a perfect arc, had just the right amount of revolutions, and dropped cleanly through the net. While the remaining Tar Heels sat on the sidelines, hunched forward, Rosenbluth skied off the bench, pumping the air with one fist.

Now, with a 53–53 tie, McGuire dropped Kearns and Cunningham back toward midcourt. He wanted to prevent any easy fast-break opportunities should the second shot miss.

But it didn't. It was equally perfect. Carolina held a 54–53 lead.

"Once the first one went in," Quigg remembers, "the second one was automatic."

Harp signaled for a timeout, losing one second in the process. The clock showed five seconds remaining. Because they had thrown the ball inbounds before calling the timeout, rules of the era allowed the Jayhawks to inbound the ball from midcourt rather than the far baseline. It was a significant difference: Five seconds was not enough time to take the ball the length of the floor and get a good shot, but it was plenty of time to dump the ball to Chamberlain from midcourt.

"The play we called was simple," Waugh says of the Kansas strategy. "We wanted to flash Loneski to the top half of the free throw circle. Wilt was going to move across the lane, and Loneski would throw it to Wilt. We knew he would either be fouled or make something good happen."

McGuire had outlined exactly the same thing to his team in the previous timeout.

King stood at the midcourt line as a decoy. Lotz first went to the corner to guard his man, leaving Quigg isolated. Quigg stood behind Chamberlain, screaming, "Danny, get in here! Get in here!"

Most of the crowd stayed politely seated. Standing at sporting events was still reserved mostly for halftime and after the game.

The ball was lobbed to Loneski, who was exactly where he was supposed to be—the middle of the foul circle, 17 feet from the basket. As he jumped to catch the ball, he turned his head to look inside at Chamberlain's position. The star had backed Quigg under the basket, just a couple feet from the hoop. The high-low play looked open.

Loneski flipped the ball inside. It was a high pass, but not too high for Chamberlain. Quigg wriggled his way around the Big Dipper and leaped to his full extension. He knew that it was a daring play. If he failed to make the interception, Chamberlain was going to be wide open. At best the Tar Heels might be able to foul him and force him to shoot free throws. At worst he would make an easy layup at the buzzer.

"The pass was underthrown," Quigg says. "I thought I had a chance to tip it, but I knew that if I missed it, we were in trouble, because Wilt was going to score. If it was even 1 inch too high, we were probably going to lose the game."

Quigg extended his left arm, hoping for the best. Then he felt leather on his fingertips and whacked the ball as hard as he could. Even if he knocked it out of bounds and gave Kansas another throw-in opportunity, he couldn't allow Chamberlain to come down with the ball. The Jayhawk reserves stood as they saw their play breaking down.

Their least favorite Tar Heel, Kearns, was standing near the sideline as the play unfolded. Suddenly, the ball was coming toward him— and so were two Jayhawks. The timing was critical.

"I knew they had five seconds when the play began," Kearns remembers. "So I knew there wasn't much time left at all. And I thought if I could throw the ball high enough, the game would be over by the time it came down."

Kearns avoided a potential steal by Parker, who wasn't aggressive enough in trying to create a clock-stopping foul. He wrapped both hands around the ball and heaved it toward the rafters. When it came down North Carolina was the 1957 NCAA men's basketball champion.

Everything had changed.

Chapter 15

The Homecoming

A little after one o'clock in the morning on Sunday, March 24, 1957, a form of mass hysteria appeared to seize the citizens of North Carolina. In cities, towns and villages all across the state, people suddenly rushed out of their houses and began to dance in the streets. Yelling at the top of their lungs, they built bonfires in the public squares. School and firehouse bells rang out, and hastily assembled street bands blared rousing southern marches.

That is how writer Gerald Holland described the postchampionship scene in *Sports Illustrated*. The euphoria was greatest in Chapel Hill. As soon as the game ended, students poured out of the student union and dashed to Franklin Street.

"I was one of the first ones out of there," says Cobby Reaves, who was a Carolina undergrad at the time. "I ran out and I couldn't believe it—the streets were bare. I didn't see a single person, and there were no cars at all. I started running up the hill towards the post office. And all of a sudden, it seemed like people were almost coming out of the ground. Before I could get to the corner of Columbia Street, the place was packed. I remember looking up and seeing people hanging out of trees and on the side of lampposts. It was incredible how quickly it filled up."

The crowd was eventually estimated at 2,000 people; this crush of humanity severely limited traffic on Franklin Street, one of the main town thoroughfares. Holland recorded a particularly curious scene: "The biggest bonfire of all was ignited smack in the middle of Franklin Street. It was down this same Franklin Street that an especially jubilant man was seen to come riding through the thick of the traffic and the snake dancers. He stood out because he was riding, not inside an automobile, but on top of one. As he jumped up and down and shouted and waved his arms, the crowd recognized him and gave him a special cheer. He was the chancellor of the University of North Carolina."

The chancellor even took the unusual step of allowing coeds to stay out until 2:00 a.m. to celebrate the victory. It was a monumental concession, but it was a monumental game.

Students infiltrated University United Methodist Church and secured hymnals and chairs to provide fuel for the raging bonfire. At any other time it might have seemed blasphemous. At the moment, though, it seemed absolutely necessary. Extra police had been dispatched to keep the crowd under control. As one cop stood next to a fellow officer, he surveyed the scene and could think of only one suitable comparison.

"Why," he said, "this is worse than V-J Day."

O

In Kansas City Carolina's celebration echoed in Municipal Auditorium. It was late, and many spectators were already putting on their coats as Tommy Kearns's heave returned to earth from its flight. The victorious players rushed toward their bench, eager to celebrate with Lennie Rosenbluth, Frank McGuire, and the rest of the squad. A handful of Tar Heel fans stormed the court, trying to become part of the fun.

NCAA officials erected a small table near center court from which to hand out tournament awards. Every Jayhawk received a runner-up trophy. Wilt Chamberlain's name was one of the first to be called. He walked toward midcourt, exchanged handshakes, and then trudged back to the Kansas bench with his head bowed. Despite his size, at that moment he looked like a youth league player who had just lost a big game.

Most of the Tar Heels pulled on their snazzy navy warm-up jackets while they waited for the championship ceremony. One by one their names were called, each player receiving some hollow cheers in the rapidly emptying arena. Buck Freeman and McGuire were the last to be recognized. McGuire, style-conscious as always, clutched at his jacket as he accepted his trophy. He couldn't resist one last tug at his tie.

And then it was over.

The Jayhawks reassembled in their locker room one final time.

"It was a tomb," Waugh recalls. "We were devastated. Any time you lose a championship, the losing side is going to be very upset. But the way it happened was so painful.

"It was even worse for Dick Harp. He took so much of the loss on himself and saw it as a personal failure. He was a fine coach and had a good year with those kids, but all he was thinking about was how he had failed them in the championship game."

"I've never seen a locker room in my life where people were so devastated," longtime *Lawrence Journal-World* writer Bill Mayer told Robert Allen Cherry, the author of *Wilt: Larger Than Life*. "There's Wilt, there's Parker and King, and Dick Harp breaks down in tears. The guys who were on that team will tell you that they have never gotten over the pain of that moment."

On that night, though, both teams quickly realized that few people outside Municipal Auditorium had any idea that an all-time classic college basketball game had just been played. Because of the cramped locker-room facilities, both teams decided to walk back to their hotels before changing clothes. It was after midnight in rainy Kansas City, and suddenly two groups of unusually tall young men were spilling onto the streets.

Chamberlain had placed a small British driving cap on his head, where it looked oddly out of place. Even in their warm-ups, other players drew little attention. Chamberlain, however, was a curiosity piece everywhere he went. (Being 7 feet tall had its advantages on the basketball court, but it could be problematic in public.) So it wasn't unusual that as he began his walk, an enthusiastic young Tar Heel fan ran by him screaming, "We wilted the Stilt!"

That was more celebrating than the Tar Heels felt like doing. They were excited, of course, but they were also exhausted. They had just finished 110 minutes of basketball in about 30 hours, without the benefit of long television timeouts. Fully a quarter of their 32 victories had been by 5 points or fewer. On three separate occasions in the past month, they had been one possession away from watching their dream of a perfect season end.

There was no champagne for Carolina. What most of the players would have liked to do was pull up a chair in the Goody Shop and kick back with Spiro Dorton and other locals who had relished every second of the six overtimes in two days. But they were a thousand miles away. McGuire invited his players to his suite for a victory celebration, but they were typical college kids who wanted to celebrate on their own rather than be surrounded by adults. Maybe, they told the coach, they would stop by his suite later in the evening.

Several team members tried to stop in a pub near the arena for a quick beer on the way back to the hotel. But the late hour—and the Carolina logo on their jackets—worked against them. Owners first indicated that they would stay open, then changed their minds and asked the Tar Heels to leave. Once they were cast back into the streets, the next choice seemed obvious: find McGuire, make use of his warm hotel room, and hope that he had excellent dinner plans.

After showering and dressing in their usual sharp blazers and ties, the team reassembled in McGuire's room. Only one person, Danny Lotz, had called his parents. It was past midnight on the East Coast, and many of the players' parents had to work on Sunday. For now the Tar Heels would have to enjoy the achievement with their basketball family.

"It was very compelling, because you had all these great basketball minds exchanging their points of view," Bob Young remembers. "It was really something to have not just our coach, but other coaches talking about the game we had just played. It was very memorable."

One of those coaches was Dean Smith, who was so depressed by his alma mater's loss that he had turned down dinner invitations in favor of returning to the hotel to indulge his misery.

Surrounded by his team and his coaching brethren, McGuire was jubilant. He asked each of his suitemates to address the team. For Ben Carnevale and Bob Spear, the request was no problem; they had rooted for the Tar Heels the entire evening. It was more challenging for Smith.

"Coach, I really don't feel like talking to your team tonight," he told McGuire, his second example of brutal honesty on the day of the championship game.

But McGuire insisted. Realizing that he was going to have to say something, Smith kept his words short and to the point: "You guys had it at the end. Congratulations. But I certainly wasn't cheering for you."

McGuire was unfazed by Smith's bluntness. In fact, he turned to the Emporia, Kansas, native—by default, the room's resident expert on local cuisine—and cheerfully asked where the team might get something to eat that late at night. Smith knew that McGuire paid little heed to the limit on his expense account; the younger coach therefore suggested Eddy's, a combination nightclub/restaurant on the corner of 13th and Baltimore, just 2 blocks from the hotel.

Eddy's was famous for being a place where diners could eat steak or lobster while enjoying some of the biggest pop acts of the era. Jerry Vale performed there; so did The Four Lads and Bill Haley and His Comets. How big a deal was Eddy's? Owner George Eddy would later turn down Barbra Streisand when a booking agent sent him a photo of the new singer. ("We'd never book anyone that ugly," Eddy said.)

He had earned the right to be picky. Supper clubs were big business; Eddy's was part of a circuit that included the Copacabana in New York City, Chez Paul in Chicago, and the Chase Club in St. Louis. Jackets were required, and the dining room could be kept open late for special circumstances—meaning people with the right connections. McGuire had those connections. He immediately arranged for the entire traveling party, including the media, to eat at Eddy's. Smith joined the group and marveled when McGuire announced, "Order anything you want."

(At that moment it seemed like Carolina basketball was poised for limitless opportunity. Soon after returning to Chapel Hill, however, McGuire learned exactly what his limits might be. Upon reviewing the expense account, athletic director Chuck Erickson scoffed at the $48 charge for Roquefort dressing. "I'm not paying that part," he informed McGuire. The Carolina head coach remembered this slight for 25 years—until 1982, when Carolina won its next national championship and then–athletic director John Swofford sent him a check to cover the cost.)

Governor Luther Hodges joined the happy crowd, this time as a warmly welcomed visitor rather than a bench interloper. Hodges had what many observers saw as a wacky idea: He wanted to turn his state, known primarily for agriculture and tobacco, into a technologically respected region. With the move of Wake Forest to Winston-Salem, the trio of Duke, Carolina, and NC State was already being referred to as "The Triangle." Hodges wanted to expand on that definition by creating the world's largest research park. He would call it the Research Triangle Park, and he believed that it would attract business and technology from all over the world.

Reaction was skeptical. But behind the slogan "Let's Get Rolling," Hodges had cultivated a core group of believers. Earlier in the school year, respected Carolina professor George L. Simpson Jr. had left the University to take over the directorship of the Governor's Research Triangle Committee. At the time, the stated goal of the committee was simple: "to increase the industrial side of the state's economy through the use of the concentration of research facilities and people at UNC, State, and Duke."

Hodges knew that his idea was only as good as the attention it could garner. He had succeeded in spreading the word throughout the state of North Carolina, but the idea was supposed to spread nationally, and eventually worldwide. He needed some way to draw positive attention to the state so that he could build off the momentum. Now he was sitting at a dinner table with the sparks of that attention.

"You guys have just done an extraordinary thing for the state of North Carolina," he told the players and their coaches, his deeper meaning unstated.

They hadn't particularly meant to do something extraordinary. But as they sat at Eddy's, wearing their dress blue travel blazers and enjoying the city's finest steak, some allowed themselves to think, just for a moment, that it might be true.

○

In theory the 1957 national champions would return to Chapel Hill as a team—conquering heroes coming home to greet their adoring fans, all of whom had stayed up past midnight the evening before to watch their team beat Kansas.

But that wasn't how it happened. Rosenbluth and McGuire were summoned to appear on *The Ed Sullivan Show*. After changing its name from *The Toast of the Town* in 1955, the program was becoming a Sunday night staple on the television landscape. It was a true variety show—only rarely was the entire hour devoted to one topic. More often, the show featured guests from a cross section of American culture.

On March 24, 1957, show producers wanted to include figures from the triple-overtime NCAA championship game. In all likelihood the player they really wanted was Wilt Chamberlain. He was nationally known and had relevance to most of the viewing public. But when the Jayhawks lost the title game, the producers cast a wider net and extended invitations to not only Chamberlain, but also New Yorkers Rosenbluth and McGuire. Sunday morning, the duo was booked on a flight that would have them in the city to appear on the show that evening. They played a relatively minor role, as they were simply seated in the audience and asked to rise so that the crowd could applaud them during one segment. But it was a major publicity coup for North Carolina basketball to have two of its own featured on one of the nation's most-watched television shows.

Before departing for the airport, McGuire had one last meal with his cronies. Just hours removed from his greatest coaching triumph, he was making plans for the next season. Freeman and McGuire had already had some frank discussions about Freeman's future in the coaching business, as the basketball lifer was prepared to hang up his whistle within the next year. Freeman was not in good health and still needed to conquer his battles with alcohol. He wasn't sure whether he would retire before the 1957–58 season, but was certain that he wouldn't coach beyond it.

That left McGuire in need of an assistant coach. With Smith still preoccupied by the fate of his beloved Jayhawks, the wily McGuire sprung a final surprise at breakfast.

"Dean, I've been talking to Ben, Hoyt, and Bob about you, and we're all in agreement," he said. "I would like for you to come to North Carolina to be my assistant coach. What do you say?"

The question stunned Smith. He wasn't expecting a job offer; in fact, he was still concerned that some of his bluntness might have cost him favor with McGuire. Now the suave leader was asking him to coach with him. Thankfully, McGuire didn't need an immediate answer. He told Smith that the offer would be open for another year if Freeman decided to return for the 1957–58 season, and the odd couple made plans to stay in touch in the weeks and months to follow.

McGuire left for the airport knowing that he had laid the groundwork for the future of his staff. What he didn't know was that he also had laid the groundwork for the future of Carolina basketball.

Rosenbluth and McGuire ended up on the same morning flight out of New York as Chamberlain. Their seats were near each other, putting the Carolina twosome in the awkward position of chatting with the player they had just defeated (and, Chamberlain may have thought, embarrassed with the tip-off stunt). Despite the loss Chamberlain had received the tournament's Most Outstanding Player award. He was just the third player from a losing team to win it in the 17-year history of the NCAA Tournament, but that fact was small consolation.

"We talked a little bit," Rosenbluth recalls. "Not much. He just said what a great game we had played and said that we had played it smart."

The Eastern Airlines flight carrying the rest of the team back to Raleigh-Durham Airport via Washington, D.C., was considerably livelier. Many of the other passengers had no knowledge of the exploits of their tall seatmates—there were no outward signs of a championship because manager Joel Fleishman had stuffed the title trophy, a silver urn, in the laundry bag with the dirty socks and uniforms. But when the pilot used the intercom system to welcome the 1957 national champions, the players received a healthy round of applause. Even the serious-minded Freeman was in good spirits. At one point he pretended to be a flight attendant and helped the stewardesses serve the in-flight lunch.

In the confines of their plane, thousands of feet above the ground, no one in the traveling party had any idea what was happening in Raleigh. Eighteen miles from Chapel Hill, the biggest traffic jam in North Carolina history was building outside the airport.

"I was absolutely amazed," says Buzz Merritt, a Carolina sports information assistant who stayed in Chapel Hill to watch the games and wanted to greet the team at the airport. "I don't even think there had been a concerted effort to get people to go to the airport. It just happened, and that was what made it more amazing. We ended up parking on the side of the highway, leaving our car, and walking the rest of the way."

Associated Press reports would later confirm that by the time the plane landed, a solid line of cars stretched from the airport back to Chapel Hill. The throng nearly caused the plane to be diverted; pilots briefly considered going to a different airport because the crowd had created safety concerns by surging onto the runway. Eventually, the well-wishers were persuaded to back up long enough to let the plane land. As the aircraft puttered low enough to give its passengers a visual of the ground, they gasped.

"The pilot had told us what was going on, but I don't think any of us envisioned what we saw when we looked out the window," Kearns recollects. "It was extraordinary. We were just kids from New York who played basketball. We went to Chapel Hill, we had a good coach, and all of a sudden we're on TV playing a triple overtime on Friday night and a triple overtime on Saturday night. And we had captured the imagination of these people in North Carolina. Overnight, we had gone from being kids from the Bronx and Brooklyn to being heroes."

Joe Quigg commandeered several strips of bacon from the onboard kitchen. Prior to the team's departure for Kansas City, one of the Carolina catchphrases had been "Bring home the bacon." Now he intended to show the adoring fans that the team had literally followed that directive.

Quigg and Pete Brennan were the first two players through the door, with Quigg waving the bacon above his head to raucous cheers from the crowd. Cars honked, thousands cheered, and the players standing behind Quigg and Brennan on the plane marveled at the noise. The crowd was estimated at 10,000.

"It was crazy," Merritt says, "but not riotous. It was just a mass of people who were all deliriously happy. It made it even better that the team got off the plane looking so classy. They just looked like they had done something important."

At that exact moment an aspiring writer named Frank Deford was traveling through North Carolina on his way home to Baltimore. He was preparing to graduate from high school and had gone to Ft. Lauderdale with a friend as a spring break treat.

"We were trying to find something on the radio," Deford recalls. "On every channel we heard the same thing: 'Here comes Quigg! Now here's Brennan!' We switched around looking for something different. And on every station in the whole damned state of North Carolina, every single radio station was covering this basketball team getting off an airplane."

After signing endless autographs, shaking countless hands, and walking through a hail of signs and confetti, the Tar Heels eventually made their way back to Chapel Hill, where they were greeted by another crowd—this one made up largely of students who had partied until late the night before and couldn't rouse themselves in time to join the swarm at the airport—outside Woollen Gym.

The only people pretending to be unimpressed were Danny Lotz's suitemates. They had traveled to Woollen to welcome the team but arrived late and ended up on the periphery of the celebration. They couldn't fathom that their Danny, the same guy with whom they had sat on a bed in the dorm and discussed the mythical figure named Wilt Chamberlain, was now a celebrity. So they returned to Cobb Dorm and went to their individual rooms, leaving every door open so that it would be obvious that they were studying.

About a half hour later, Lotz charged through the front door with a broad smile on his face. He had been greeted royally by fans and expected the same from his friends. Instead, he was greeted with . . . nothing. He peeked in the first room and saw a classmate engrossed in a textbook.

"Hi, guys," Lotz said. "I'm back."

"Oh. Hi, Dan," came the reply.

The same conversation was repeated at each room, with Lotz growing more perplexed by the moment. He was the lone Tar Heel who had spoken to his parents; he, perhaps more than anyone on the team, knew what a frenzy the win had caused in the state of North Carolina. Was his dorm the only place unaffected by the impact?

He went to his room, where suddenly he heard the sound of muffled laughter. His roommates had been able to maintain the charade for only about five minutes. Soon, they were piling into his room, firing off questions about Chamberlain, Kansas City, and being a national champion.

As for Quigg, he soon discovered that he was no longer known as the campus's tallest tobacco representative. The night he arrived back in Chapel Hill, he had a long-scheduled date. He and the lucky coed walked into the Varsity Theater on Franklin Street early, well before the lights were dimmed.

"We were walking down the aisle to find a seat, and everybody in the theater got up and started clapping," Quigg says now. "I about died. I turned all shades of red. It was one thing to have fans cheering you, but this was mostly my peers."

The next week, he had the same experience with a group that was made up entirely of peers. His zoology professor had scheduled a quiz for the Friday after the championship. Quigg was nervous because this was one of his toughest classes, and the time he would have devoted to studying had been spent flying to and from basketball arenas.

The professor stood at the lectern on Friday morning and asked for the class's attention. "In honor of the national championship, we're putting the test off until next class," he said.

Quigg felt almost as much relief as he had in Kansas City after making the two title-clinching free throws.

Basketball stayed on the front page of the *Daily Tar Heel* sports section for most of the week. By the following Thursday, though, it had been supplanted by a different banner headline: ORGANIZED ANTI-NEGRO PROBLEM TO BE ENDED IN FIFTY YEARS, SAYS MALIN. The story referenced a recent speech by Patrick Murphy Malin, the head of the American Civil Liberties Union, who would grow that organization's membership from 9,000 to 60,000 during his tenure. Malin had told his Chapel Hill audience that the oppression faced by African Americans would be a distant memory by 2007. By then, he thought, racial divisions would be as quaint as horse-drawn carriages.

In that same issue of the paper was a small news item titled ROSEN-BLUTH TO WED. It was now campuswide news that the star of the most famous team in Carolina intercollegiate athletics history was engaged to Helen Powell Oliver of Mount Airy, with the ceremony to take place just a few days hence, on June 1. Despite its attention to this tidbit, the *Daily Tar Heel* editorial board still wasn't convinced of the merits of basketball.

"Is this basketball fever a good thing or a bad thing?" the paper asked in a staff editorial. "Properly regulated, it is a good thing. But one word of caution is in order. Carolina's success will stimulate interest in basketball all the way down to the grammar school level. In the future, North Carolina colleges who want to retain popular favor would do well to devote more attention to homegrown talent."

The Tar Heels were not concerned that, in some quarters, they were still seen as the intruders from New York. They had other appointments to keep, including one at the governor's mansion, where Luther Hodges was still riding the wave of popularity enjoyed by his new favorite basketball team. Many players were flummoxed by the elaborate table settings at the governor's home. They were accustomed to needing one, or at most two, forks. Now they were faced with enough silverware to stock a department store. The menu that evening included quail.

"I just looked at it," Kearns remembers. "Of course I had never had quail before. The stuff still had buckshot in it. I just remember thinking one thing: 'What the hell is this?'"

It was the first tangible sign of the way the players' lives had changed. They had gone from anonymously cramming into two station wagons for road games to dining on quail with the governor.

The championship contest was, as some people on campus seemed intent on reminding them, just a basketball game. But it was more than that.

It was a life-changing basketball game.

Chapter 16
The
Aftermath

For the most part the people touched by North Carolina's 1957 national championship thrived in the spotlight. They also found themselves strangely connected by the events that took place in Municipal Auditorium on March 23, 1957.

Frank McGuire coached at Carolina until the end of the 1960–61 season. When he left he retained the shine of the title, but he was restless and needed a new opportunity. His lavish dinners for the media and other friends were coming under scrutiny, and the athletic department was no longer willing to humor his lack of attention to detail.

McGuire took a job with the Philadelphia Warriors, where one of his star players was a promising center named Wilt Chamberlain. McGuire guided the team to the Eastern Conference finals of the 1961–62 season, all the while joking that his primary responsibility was to make sure Chamberlain knew what time to be on the team plane. But the coach's most memorable moment came on the night of March 2, 1962, when the big center scored 100 points in a single game in Hershey, Pennsylvania.

The Warriors moved to California after that season, but McGuire refused to go with them. He returned to college coaching with South Carolina in 1964, putting him in the same conference with his former employer. He stayed with the Gamecocks until 1980 and was a party to numerous heated battles between North and South Carolina. (The 1971 ACC Tournament championship game between the two rivals remains an all-time classic tournament contest.) In 1977 the Gamecocks renamed their basketball facility Frank McGuire Arena. McGuire was inducted into the Basketball Hall of Fame that same year.

Nothing in Chapel Hill was ever named for McGuire, but he may have made an even greater contribution to Carolina basketball than the 1957 national championship. Buck Freeman did stay with the Tar Heels one more year after the title; when he retired, Dean Smith accepted McGuire's invitation to become an assistant coach. During Smith's first season in that position, McGuire went on a five-day recruiting trip to New York and left Smith in charge of practice. By the time the head coach returned, Smith had installed a completely new defense—the point zone, which would become the primary defense of the 1959 Tar Heels and a major component of McGuire's book *Defensive Basketball*. Over his next two seasons with the team, Smith continued to gain the respect of the Carolina administration.

When the NCAA sanctioned the Carolina basketball program in 1960 for excessive recruiting expenditures—sanctions that included the elimination of Harry Gotkin as a go-between to New York prospects—it was Smith who was appointed to compile the paperwork for the school's appeal. NCAA council members were impressed with Carolina's presentation, noting that they had "never heard a more thorough and detailed defense of a university's position than we did today." Nevertheless, the sanctions were upheld, and the Tar Heels were placed on one year of probation. Chancellor William Aycock notified McGuire that his off-the-court performance over the next year would be critical to the renewal of his contract. Several weeks later, McGuire left for the Warriors.

McGuire recommended Smith as his replacement even though Smith might find it difficult to compete at Carolina under the cloud of additional university-imposed sanctions, due partially to a gambling scandal centered at NC State. These restrictions included limiting the recruitment of players from outside the ACC region to two per year. McGuire's concerns were allayed by the granite support of Aycock, who saw Smith through several crises early in his career.

The man who had once slept on a cot in McGuire's hotel room went on to become the winningest coach in the history of Division I men's college basketball, a title he held until 2007. He won national championships in 1982 and 1993 and watched as Carolina named its palatial 21,000-seat basketball arena after him in 1986.

(He still keeps an office in the Smith Center, where he stays in touch with every former player and answers an ever-flowing stream of fan mail.)

Smith was equally important to UNC off the court. After a game at Woollen Gym, McGuire was once asked if he would be interested in integrating Atlantic Coast Conference basketball. He was not a bigot, but he also dealt in realities—and the reality was that integration at UNC would have been very difficult in the mid-1950s. His response to the question was a gentle shrug. "Not me," he said. "I'm not going to be the first one."

Smith's approach was entirely different. In the early 1960s, while still an assistant coach, he joined with Binkley Baptist Church pastor Robert Seymour to integrate The Pines, where McGuire had once wanted to hold weekly press conferences. Congress had just passed the Public Accommodations law; Seymour wanted to see how committed Chapel Hill establishments were to upholding it. Seymour and Smith escorted a black student to the restaurant, where the three patrons were promptly served.

O

With the nucleus of Joe Quigg and his junior teammates returning to campus, the Tar Heels were expected to be national contenders again in 1958. But Quigg broke his leg in a freak preseason accident and sat out the entire season. As it turned out, the last shots of his college basketball career were the two championship-clinching free throws against Kansas. The New York Knicks drafted him in 1958, but his leg did not heal adequately enough to allow him to play professional ball, either.

If any Tar Heel had to sustain a career-ending injury, Quigg probably was best suited for the challenge. He knew throughout college that he wanted to be a dentist, and he achieved that goal, working in the profession until his retirement in 2000. He and his wife, Carol, have lived in Fayetteville, North Carolina, since 1966. Over the last four decades, he has developed the slightest hint of a Southern accent.

Lennie Rosenbluth was expected to have the best professional career of any of the Tar Heels. He left Carolina holding every major scoring record and was picked by the Warriors in the 1957 draft. But he found the roster at his position well stocked—Philadelphia already had eventual Hall of Famer Paul Arizin. Rosenbluth's slender build caused him problems in the physical pro game, and he played just two pro seasons.

He did marry Pat Oliver on June 1, 1957. As a wedding present Spiro Dorton handed Rosenbluth a fistful of receipts from the Goody

Shop. The basketball star had been signing tabs there for four years and paying them off whenever he received a small allowance from his parents.

"You don't have to pay these anymore," Dorton told him. "Start your new life with no debt."

Rosenbluth gave the stack of tabs to his little brother. Several years later, he discovered what had happened to them—his brother had sold them, one at a time. Ordinary receipts signed by the great Lennie Rosenbluth went for a quarter apiece.

Rosenbluth spent several successful years as a high school basketball coach in Florida. At one time he tutored a talented point guard named Chris Corchiani and encouraged this fellow to play in the Atlantic Coast Conference. Rosenbluth watched as Corchiani went on to become one of the NCAA's all-time leading assist men . . . for NC State.

Lennie and Pat Rosenbluth still live in Florida, although they make a yearly pilgrimage to Chapel Hill to attend a handful of basketball games.

Along with Bob Cunningham, Pete Brennan—who would leave Chapel Hill an accomplished player—entered the business world. After long and successful careers, both men found the pull of the South too much to overcome. In fall 2005 Brennan organized a wildly successful reunion of the 1957 team on North Carolina's Outer Banks; he is a regular at the Smith Center for home games. (Memories of his lucky Chrysler remain, even though it was towed from its spot in front of the Monogram Club within days of Carolina's victory over Kansas.) Cunningham passed away in June 2006 after battling cancer.

Bob Young splits his time between New York and Florida; Joel Fleishman is in the clothing business in Greensboro. Danny Lotz became a successful dentist and runs a popular Bible study group in Chapel Hill. Ken Rosemond worked as Smith's assistant before ascending to the head coaching position at Georgia. (He was on the team bus the January night in 1965 that Smith was famously hung in effigy by angry Carolina students.) Like Fleishman, Rosemond eventually entered the clothing business. He died five days after Carolina won the 1993 national championship.

Woody Durham graduated from the University of North Carolina six years after he watched the 1957 title game with his father. He became the play-by-play radio announcer for Carolina in 1971 and has held the position ever since.

C. D. Chesley, who had worked so hard to broadcast the 1957 NCAA semifinal game against Michigan State, built an ACC television empire. Beginning in 1958, he inaugurated the practice of airing an ACC Game of the Week. It became a regional phenomenon as a generation of fans—all of whom knew the trademark "Sail with the Pilot" jingle coined by broadcast sponsor Pilot Life Insurance—learned to set aside their Saturday afternoons for the latest basketball clash.

Basketball in North Carolina evolved from a cultural passion to big business. There has not been a public sale of ACC Tournament tickets since 1966. Boosters are now required to donate thousands of dollars (at some schools, including at North Carolina, the figure is closer to hundreds of thousands of dollars) just for the privilege of buying the precious tickets. The conference tournament is the culmination of a season-long televised basketball smorgasbord. In the first three years after his return to Carolina, Roy Williams coached the Tar Heels in 98 basketball games. All but three games were televised. During the 2005–06 season, a record 276 games involving ACC teams were televised.

For Wilt Chamberlain the 1957 championship game began a career in which he realized that the world never fully loves a giant. Every year from 1991 to 1997, Kansas tried to retire his jersey, but Chamberlain did not respond to the invitations. He disliked ritual, but he also was unsure what reaction he would receive in a town that had felt stung by his early departure from college in 1958. He finally acquiesced in 1998. Even as he walked onto the Allen Fieldhouse court for a halftime ceremony, he told an acquaintance, "I hope they don't boo me."

They didn't boo. They cheered long and loud. He addressed the crowd only briefly, but his opening remarks spoke volumes: "A little over 40 years ago, I lost my toughest battle in sports in losing to the North Carolina Tar Heels by 1 point in triple overtime. It was a devastating thing to me because I thought I let the university down and my teammates down."

His sentiments were not a surprise to most of the Tar Heels. Also in the late 1990s, a group of former Tar Heels, including Cunningham and Rosenbluth, gathered in Boca Raton, Florida. They stopped in a club that Chamberlain owned on Glades Road.

"We're here to see Wilt Chamberlain," they said.

The hostess explained that the owner wasn't in town on that particular day. Rosenbluth drew himself to his full height and walked to the hostess stand.

"Would you mind telling him," he asked politely, "that Lennie Rosenbluth is here to see him?"

The hostess disappeared. Almost immediately, she reappeared—with Chamberlain. The group talked late into the night, and the conversation inevitably turned to 1957.

"I played a lot of basketball games," Chamberlain told the group. "And of all of them, that game against North Carolina was the one I really wanted to win."

Legendary *Sports Illustrated* journalist Frank Deford got to know Chamberlain well when their careers in sports intersected.

"In terms of Wilt, that game would have changed everything about him," Deford says. "He never would have been stamped as a loser, even if he had lost games the next couple of years. He probably would not have left college early. I think he would have felt better about himself just by virtue of having this on his resume. He would have been able to say, 'I beat an undefeated team. Nobody else could do it, but they gave us a close game, and I did it.'

"The attitude about Wilt Chamberlain in his early pro years would have been unmistakably different."

One of the most unlikely friendships to emerge from the 1957 championship game was that between Chamberlain and Tommy Kearns. They had been opponents in the center jump circle on that memorable night, the big man embarrassed that the little man stood opposite him. Kearns later began a very successful career as a stockbroker, and eventually he was reintroduced to Chamberlain. They became close friends, often meeting at Chamberlain's home in California to share expensive wine.

Kearns is one of the few 1957 Tar Heels who has thus far resisted the siren call of the South. He is a New Yorker to the core, splitting his time between New York City and his home in Connecticut. In the city he can sometimes get through business meetings without acquaintances piecing together his background as a college basketball pioneer. In North Carolina, however, his name remains golden.

"When Frank [Deford] wrote an article on the '57 team, he said that jumping center was my defining moment," Kearns reflects. "And I think that's true for all of us. When they write our obituaries, that's going to be near the top. Life goes on, and new kids are always coming along. But one of the chapters in all our lives will always be that season, and we're always going to be teammates."

Epilogue

Frank McGuire was impeccably dressed, as always. His tie was pulled tight to his spread collar, his jacket perfectly tailored. His auburn hair was slicked back. He looked like an ad for a clothing store.

It was the fall of 1957, and he was standing in front of a room of boys who thought he was the king of the basketball world.

Maybe they were right. He was just a few months removed from leading the University of North Carolina to the NCAA basketball championship, the first in the school's history. He had revived a program that before his arrival had been a distant second to North Carolina State in the Atlantic Coast Conference. He had students on the UNC campus chattering about the game of basketball, to the point that the sport with the round ball could at least come close to claiming the same popularity as football.

He stood in front of the boys of Chi Psi not as a coach, but as a hero.

This is what he said: "In the future, there will be other good basketball teams. People will want to compare those teams to our 1957 North Carolina team. When you hear people make that comparison, you need to say, 'OK, when that team goes through the regular season undefeated and then goes through the ACC Tournament undefeated and then goes through the NCAA Tournament undefeated, then you can start to compare them.'

"Every team wins a championship every year. But to win it the way our 1957 team did, that's going to be very difficult. That's what is going to make that team different from all other teams in the future. That's what makes them the best."

1956–57 North Carolina Tar Heels Final Roster

(as of 3/23/57)

No.	Name	Pos.	Age	Ht.	Wt.	Class	Hometown
10	Lennie Rosenbluth	F	23	6-5	180	Sr.	Bronx, NY
35	Pete Brennan	F	20	6-6	190	Jr.	Brooklyn, NY
33	Danny Lotz	F	19	6-7	198	Soph.	Northport, NY
22	Roy Searcy	F	20	6-4	185	Jr.	Draper, NC
31	Gehrmann Holland	F	19	6-3	200	Soph.	Beaufort, NC
41	Joe Quigg	C	20	6-9	210	Jr.	Brooklyn, NY
20	Bob Young	C	21	6-6	220	Sr.	Queens, NY
40	Tommy Kearns	G	20	5-11	191	Jr.	Bergenfield, NJ
32	Bob Cunningham	G	20	6-4	190	Jr.	New York City, NY
11	Ken Rosemond	G	26	5-10	155	Jr.	Hillsborough, NC

1956–57 North Carolina Tar Heels Results

Date	Opponent	Location	W/L	Score
12/4	Furman	Chapel Hill	W	94–66
12/8	Clemson	Charlotte	W	94–75
12/12	George Washington	Norfolk	W	82–55
12/15	South Carolina	Columbia	W	90–86 (OT)
12/17	Maryland	Chapel Hill	W	70–61
12/20	NYU	New York City	W	64–59
12/21	Dartmouth	Boston	W	89–61
12/22	Holy Cross	Boston	W	83–70
12/27	Utah (Dixie Classic)	Raleigh	W	97–76
12/28	Duke (DC)	Raleigh	W	87–71
12/29	Wake Forest (DC)	Raleigh	W	63–55

1/8	William & Mary	Williamsburg	W	71–61
1/11	Clemson	Chapel Hill	W	86–54
1/12	Virginia	Chapel Hill	W	102–90
1/15	NC State	Raleigh	W	83–57
1/30	Western Carolina	Cullowhee	W	77–59
2/5	Maryland	College Park	W	65–61 (2OT)
2/9	Duke	Chapel Hill	W	75–73
2/11	Virginia	Charlottesville	W	68–59
2/13	Wake Forest	Chapel Hill	W	72–69
2/19	NC State	Chapel Hill	W	86–57
2/22	South Carolina	Chapel Hill	W	75-62
2/26	Wake Forest	Winston-Salem	W	69–64
3/1	Duke	Durham	W	86–72
3/7	Clemson (ACC Tournament)	Raleigh	W	81–61
3/8	Wake Forest (ACC)	Raleigh	W	61–59
3/9	South Carolina (ACC)	Raleigh	W	95–75
3/12	Yale (NCAA Tournament)	New York City	W	90–74
3/15	Canisius (NCAA)	Philadelphia	W	87–75
3/16	Syracuse (NCAA)	Philadelphia	W	67–58
3/22	Michigan State (NCAA)	Kansas City	W	74–70 (3OT)
3/23	Kansas (NCAA)	Kansas City	W	54–53 (3OT)

Index